The Grant Writer's Guide

How to Become an Expert Grant Writer
for Schools and Nonprofit Groups

Written by Dr. Linda Karges-Bone

Illustrated by Anita DuFalla

Good Apple
A Division of Frank Schaffer Publications, Inc.

Dedication and Message

This book is dedicated to the fine educators in Berkeley County, South Carolina, who have devoted countless hours to writing proposals and finding grant monies to improve the lives of children. Your search is not in vain. This scripture is for you: "How blessed is the man who finds wisdom and the man who gains understanding, for its profit is better than the profit of silver, and its gain than fine gold."

—Proverbs 3:13, 14

Acknowledgments

Special thanks to Douglas Rife and Donna Borst, who are great supporters of my work, and to Gwen Brock, Antonia Cappelletti, Frank Collins, Judy Dellicolli, Lynn Foes, Carolyn Gillens, Elizabeth Grooms, Gary Leonard, Eileen Maness, Pam Murray, Laura Nestor, Gloria Parker, Jane Pulling, Karen Richardson, and Kathy Sobolewski who helped to make grant writing a reality for teachers in rural schools.

Recognition

I wish to recognize the contributions of Rosalind Banks, Lynn Camlin, Frances Coull, Tracy H. Gaskins, Jane Marinacci, Linda Royce, and Amanda Upton whose sample grants are included in this book. These teachers have been generous and professional in sharing their expertise with other educators. Their grants are proof that attitude, attributes, and action result in grants that change children's lives. Thank you all.

Editors: Loretta Rooney Hess, Kristin Eclov, Christine Hood
Cover Design: Jonathan Wu
Cover Illustration: Roger Chandler
Book Design: Anthony D. Paular
Graphic Artist: Randy Shinsato

Good Apple
A Division of Frank Schaffer Publications, Inc.
23740 Hawthorne Boulevard
Torrance, CA 90505-5927

GA13054

Table of Contents

Purpose of This Book

Many of you reading this book are already familiar with its companion text, the best-selling *Grant Writing for Teachers* (Good Apple, 1994). Thousands of educators learned how to write a successful proposal after using that book, and I have been gratified by the positive response that *Grant Writing for Teachers* continues to receive.

However, since I published *Grant Writing for Teachers,* I have been amazed by two phenomena: 1) how much teachers want to learn to write grants, and 2) how eager teachers are to "get into" finding grant money. The book has sold well, but that's not the best part. The best part is that teachers around the country have been successful in writing grants. At my workshops, through e-mail, and in notes from teachers, I hear a common response: "You took the mystery out of [grant writing]!" Teachers and others involved in nonprofit programs that impact children and youth have also asked for more information and ideas on grant writing.

To meet those needs, I have created this companion book to *Grant Writing for Teachers—The Grant Writer's Guide: How to Become an Expert Grant Writer for Schools and Nonprofit Groups.* This book is timely and important because teachers insist that once they know the "nuts and bolts" of proposal design, which is addressed in the first book, they want to "develop grant writing expertise," which is the task of this book.

This book offers three new directions for educators:

- Specific ideas for dealing with common problems that make a grant go wrong. Issues such as deciding to go after private or public money, ethics of grant writing, and designing dissemination plans are covered.

- A robust directory of sources for grants, including a section on using the Internet to find grant money, is provided. You will find 51 new sources for funding.

- A section of sample grants collected from my workshops and some I wrote, as well as a sample letter of intent are included for your review. This section is highly desired by teachers. In every city where I speak, teachers say:

"Dr. Bone, I need to see a few grants. Don't you have a book with sample grants in it?" Here they are!

I was eager to do this project because teachers have asked me to do it and because there is a lack of affordable, accessible information on grant writing.

Also, the addition of "for nonprofit groups" in the title opens this book up to a whole new audience—private schools, YMCAs, youth agencies, and community agencies that have little material available to them. Anyone who works with children and youth will find this book helpful in finding funds and proposal design. *The Grant Writer's Guide: How to Become an Expert Grant Writer for Schools and Nonprofit Groups* provides useful material to many schools and agencies at a reasonable price.

As you move through this resource, consider the words from Proverbs offered in the Dedication and Message, and ask yourself how the grant you are seeking provides wisdom for yourself and for others. Your grant is not simply a vehicle for bringing in dollars; it is a way to fund change and growth, and for that you need wisdom. Good luck and feel free to contact me by e-mail at: lbone@csuniv.edu if you have questions.

Dr. Linda Karges-Bone
Charleston, South Carolina

Chapter One:
What Makes a
Grant Writer Successful?

**Words of
Wisdom**

A bashful beggar

has an empty

wallet.

—*Hungarian Saying*

Each chapter in this grant writer's guide begins with "words of wisdom" that set the tone for the message. Consider this one—"A bashful beggar has an empty wallet"—as we review the attitudes, attributes, and actions of successful grant writers.

Some folks say that getting grants is about "getting lucky." I disagree. It is not that simple. Yes, one can be in the right place at the right time, but it is no accident. Successful grant writers don't stumble onto grant dollars. Instead, they pursue a carefully thought-out route toward grant money and are usually in the right territory when the proposal gets funded. Just yesterday, for example, I heard from a school district's staff development director who had hired me to assist its teachers in pursuing some state incentive grants (see Question Two in Chapter Two, regarding private vs. public money, page 18). She was ecstatic, because the district's teachers had garnered over $125,000 in individual incentive grants. These awards ranged from $1,200 to $10,000 each, with the average grant amount in the neighborhood of $2,000, so a significant number of teachers were involved in writing grants. "Thank you so much, Dr. Bone!" she exclaimed.

"Thank your teachers," I replied. "I just gave them some guidance and encouragement. They made it happen."

How, you might ask, did these teachers become so successful in finding and writing grants? They had the right **attitude**; displayed the right **attributes**; and took the appropriate **action**. These three A's will earn you an A+ in grant writing, too!

The First "A" Is Attitude

Remember the old Hungarian saying that we began with? In grant writing, there is no room for bashfulness. Educators who want grant money must be bold, not brazen, mind you, but bold. You cannot sit around and wait for the perfect grant to fall into your lap. Take the initiative. Ask questions. Get "in the loop." Here are some of the attitudes that I have observed among successful teachers, nonprofit directors, and school administrators who find and get grants.

- Successful grant writers see grant writing as an exciting challenge, not as another task "dumped" on them.

- Successful grant writers like research and use it to underpin their proposals. Instead of asking, "How can I get money for what I want?" these folks look at the current research in education, psychology, parenting, or wellness and say, "What does the research suggest about kids and learning, and how can we use that to get grant money?"

- Successful grant writers are "out there" in their fields. They go to conferences. They read teaching magazines and trade journals. They browse bookstores and listen to public radio to find out "what's hot" and then use it in their proposal design.

- Successful grant writers love a challenge. They see the glass as half full, not half empty, and go after grant money to fill it up the rest of the way.

- Successful grant writers are positive, enthusiastic, and have a sense of humor. People like to be around them and that kind of charm goes a long way in dealing with funding sources and boards that are considering a proposal. Their sense of humor keeps them grounded, so that when a proposal is not funded, they simply shrug their shoulders and send it out to another source.

- Successful grant writers are team players. They don't try to do all the work themselves, although many of them prefer to actually write the proposal alone. For example, they delegate jobs to a grant-writing team—getting letters of support, finding research articles, making phone calls, typing lists for the budget, getting estimates and prices—but ultimately "pull it all together" themselves.

- Successful grant writers see themselves as "servants" in the purest sense of the word. They are deeply committed to their work, their students, and their mission. They view grant writing as a way to fulfill important personal goals that they have set for their work and their lives.

The Second "A" Is Attributes

You may not be born with all of the right attitudes we discussed earlier because most of these stem from one's personality. That's okay, because the "attributes" of successful grant writers are equally as important, and you can learn or develop these by modeling, listening, and applying skills.

- Successful grant writers demonstrate clear, concise written and oral communication skills. Learn how to use words carefully and skillfully. Practice finding words that you really like and fitting them into the proposal in the perfect place. "Fool around" with words. Start a list of phrases and sayings that you like. Look at the original *Grant Writing for Teachers* book, which has an entire section called "Choose the Right Word." Review the sample grants in Chapter Five (page 77) of this book to see how the writers use language.

- Successful grant writers are organized. Keep a notebook or file of grant sources and applications. Make copies of everything when you are working on a grant. Back up data on disks. Save articles and research notes that you'll use in a grant at a later date.

- Successful grant writers have a strong work ethic. They expect to put time into a grant proposal and have no patience for laziness or sloppiness in their work.

- Successful grant writers learn to use technology to their advantage. They may like yellow legal pads for brainstorming but put their proposals on a word processing program. They may keep an old-fashioned file folder of research articles but know how to browse the Internet to find funding sources or to locate an expert who can supply them with a letter of support.

- Successful grant writers display confidence and polish in their professional dealings and in "networking." Some of the techniques I have seen among solid grant-writing educators include: 1) trading business cards with other educators so they can "keep up" with people, 2) clipping newspaper articles about authors or experts on whom they might call for a letter of support, and 3) joining the Rotary Club or chamber of commerce in order to "get in the loop" for local grants and awards.

- Successful grant writers keep up with professional organizations, typically belonging to two or three national or international groups, such as the International Reading Association, National Geographic Society, or Association for Supervision and Curriculum Development.

- Successful grant writers learn to pace themselves, set deadlines, and do a little bit every day on a proposal, so they don't get stuck in a rush to put a proposal in the mail that isn't worthy and polished.

The Third "A" Is Action

- Successful grant writers go to workshops on grant writing, such as those sponsored by the National Education Institute. To get on the mailing list for a workshop in your community, you can call (715) 831-2436.

- Successful grant writers believe in and practice long-range planning. For example, they know that to get a technology grant, they will be expected to attach a five-year technology plan for their school as an addendum to the proposal.

- Successful grant writers keep up their own resumes or vitae (a special kind of resume used by teachers and other professionals who have more than a master's degree, and, perhaps, some publishing or presentation history). They know that a resume, up to date and polished, can be an important factor in getting a grant reader to pay attention to a proposal.

- Successful grant writers know that it takes many small grants to build up to a "big grant" ($10,000 or more). One doesn't start out with a big grant. One cuts one's teeth on small grants, both for practice and because larger grants usually have a required section in which the writer must describe a history of prior success. In other words, you have to have a track record before the "big funders" will look at you!

- Successful grant writers maintain good relationships with their administrators, principals, and/or boards of directors. Funding sources don't like to deal with troublemakers or agitators. They don't want to be forced to deal with your, or your agency's, internal problems. Keep your reputation unblemished and your references impeccable. (See "The Ethics of Grant Writing," page 54.) It is amazing to me the way that people know each other in the world of grants and fund-raising.

- Successful grant writers don't rush into a proposal. They get the support of their superiors. They let the school district know that they want to pursue a grant. In fact, most districts require a written "go ahead" before a teacher can apply for a grant. Make sure that you know what the rules are and that you keep everyone informed of your grant-writing plans or you may be disappointed, reprimanded, or even fired because you are perceived as a "loose cannon."

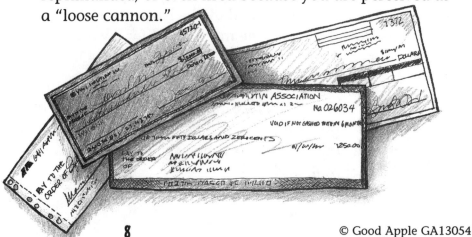

8

Those are the attitudes, attributes, and actions of successful grant writers. I have, to date, either written grants myself or helped schools and teachers write grants, which have secured over two million dollars in grant monies that I know about. I present workshops all over the country, and thousands of teachers have purchased *Grant Writing for Teachers,* so who knows how many grants have been secured using the techniques and suggestions I've shared? I hope that all of you reading this will get your grant. But remember, don't be bashful! Your attitudes, attributes, and actions have to be bold and decisive. Make the first move— just make sure that it is the *right* move. To be sure, read this book first. Look at the articles. Examine the chapter on problems in grant writing. Study the chapter on funding sources to make the right match. Try your hand at using the Internet. Decide on public or private money for your needs. Review the sample grants in Chapter Five. Be sure to read the original *Grant Writing for Teachers*, too! Then, make your move. A successful grant writer is made, not born, and you are on your way.

Date _____

Will You Be a Successful Grant Writer?

Directions: Take this quick quiz to measure your potential for success in grant writing. You may want to use this quiz as a "warm up" in a workshop for teachers on your faculty. Circle *yes* or *no*.

1. Grant writing is mostly a matter of luck, not a matter of skill.

   Yes   No

2. It is better to go after a big grant rather than to waste time on little $500 or $1,000 awards.

   Yes   No

3. Grant writing is very technical and boring; you can't put your personality into it.

   Yes   No

4. You can get a technology grant for computers or software just by describing the great need for technology in your school.

   Yes   No

5. You have to be very aggressive in grant writing, so expect to make a few enemies.

   Yes   No

6. I'm not really up on the current research in my field, but that shouldn't matter because grants are about what you need for your school, not what the latest journal article says.

   Yes   No

10

7. I'm a teacher and my classroom is what is important to me. I don't have the time or inclination to go to professional conferences and meetings.

   Yes   No

8. I prefer to work alone. Teams take up too much time and the grant would never get done.

   Yes   No

9. The best way to find grant sources is to look on the bulletin board in the lounge. If it is there and it interests me, maybe I'll work on it.

   Yes   No

10. I like to keep my ideas to myself. I would probably submit a grant secretly so that other teachers won't steal my idea and the principal won't say "no." I'll just surprise them!

    Yes   No

Rate Your Responses

- **8–10 No Responses**—You are an *A+* grant writer. You have the right attitudes, attributes, and actions in line. You should be getting, or are ready to go after, grant dollars.

- **5–7 No Responses**—You are in the *B* category. You have some good intentions and some positive skills, but you need to learn more about the grant world or you might make a critical blunder.

- **0–4 No Responses**—You get a *C* on this quiz. You probably have little or no experience in the grant world. You need to do some reading, go to a workshop, and talk to some experienced grant writers before you put pen to paper. You are in a good position because you probably have no "bad skills" to unlearn.

Date _____

Begin with Goal Setting

Directions: Set goals for becoming a more confident, successful grant writer. After reading Chapter One and taking the quiz on pages 10 and 11, write down your professional goals concerning grant writing.

1. _____

2. _____

3. _____

4. _____

5. _____

6. _____

7. _____

8. _____

9. _____

Chapter Two: Finding the Right Match for Your Idea

13

Words of Wisdom

66A good beginning

is half the work.99

—Irish Saying

In the grant world, both in finding a funding source and in writing proposals, you will find that most of your work comes "up front" in the research and planning stages. Answer the following questions before drafting a proposal:

- Does the funding source match your needs?

- Is your idea best suited to private or public grant funding?

- Is there a "geography problem"? Many funding sources limit their gifts to specific geographic regions.

- Do you have a 501-c-3 letter if you are going after private money?

- Are you working with a "hot," very fundable topic or curriculum area? Your idea may be sound and even necessary, but funding seems to follow trends. You would do well to keep up with those trends.

- Is your perspective in place? Do you let funders know that you want to try something new, not that you just want to buy a lot of stuff?

Each of these questions is answered in the following sections. There is a short section discussing the problem, and a worksheet to help you organize your action plan for dealing with the issue. Remember our words of wisdom for Chapter Two: "A good beginning is half the work." If you: (1) start off with the appropriate funding match, (2) take care to note limitations to funding, and (3) select a hot topic, your chances of funding are greatly enhanced.

Six Important Questions

Question One: How do I find the right match between a funding source and my needs?

At my grant-writing seminars around the country, teachers are often surprised to hear me say, "Grant writing is less about writing and more about research." It is true, however. One does not even write the first word of a grant narrative until one finds the right funding source, the "perfect match" for the potential grant.

Like searching for a possible spouse, finding the right match for your grant idea takes time, research, and looking in the right places. Here are the steps to finding the right match for your grant idea.

Step One: Do a *needs assessment* for your project idea. Look at current research. Interview faculty, clients, parents, and staff. Review the performance of your students or the records of your clients. Seek to understand the culture and scope of the problems in your school or agency. Then ask yourself and your colleagues, "What do we need from this grant and why do we need it?"

Also, find out if there is support for your grant among faculty, colleagues, administration, parents, and the community.

Consider the issue of leadership for the proposed program. Do you have a leader who will guide the development of the project with enthusiasm and vision? Will his or her resume, or vita, add credibility to the proposal?

These questions are critical and will influence the outcome of the grant search. Spend time with the needs assessment. Don't be lured by the glitter of possible grant dollars and overlook key questions or issues that arise from the assessment.

Step Two: Use the results of the needs assessment to formulate a working abstract for the project. An abstract is a one- to two-page summary of the project that explains succinctly and clearly what you plan to do. In the abstract, one should determine a "ball-park figure" for the budget. How much do you think it will cost to do what you want? Did you double-check with your funding guidelines to see if the source funds projects in this amount?

Step Three: Give your abstract and project a working title. The use of a title makes your project real and approachable. In Chapter Three on page 32, you will find a section on writing "tantalizing titles."

Step Four: Begin the search for the perfect match. Begin with the decision to go after private or public money. This issue is discussed in Question Two on page 18.

Step Five: Use library and Internet resources to locate one to three possible private sources for your grant and one to two possible state or federal sources. Be sure to determine the following by looking at "limitations" or "limitations to funding" information listed in the grant source. These limitations tell you whether or not you "match up" to the funding source. Ask yourself these questions: *Does the source fund your kind of school or agency? Is the source private? public? religious? nonprofit? Does the source fund grants in the dollar amount you need? Do they fund grants in your state or region?* (See Question Three on page 21.) *Are they currently accepting new applications? Does the source require matching funds?* That means that you will have to have a dollar match in the budget. You have to show money up front via a letter of support.

You will find the answers to these questions in the section marked "Limitations to Funding," which is found in the grant sourcebook or Internet site that you are using, or in the project guidelines. Typically, one approaches a foundation or other funding source by calling or writing for a "packet" on grants, in which you will receive the following: (1) project guidelines (what you have to do and what they will fund), (2) application forms and data, and (3) a copy of the group's annual report (a mission statement, board of directors, and a list of previously funded grants).

Look carefully over every piece of information in the packet. All of it can help you to decide if this source is a match for you and how to proceed with the proposal design if you are a match.

For example, by reviewing the annual report, you can find out the following critical information:

- Do you have any valuable contacts or connections among board members? You would be surprised at the names that show up on these boards. Did you go to college with someone on the board? Do you know a businessperson or legislator on the board? A religious leader? A carefully placed phone call or note could help you out.

- Does the group's mission statement fit with your own? Do you have much in common with this group?

- Check out the list and description of previously funded projects. Do they seem to fund projects that are similar to what you propose?

Step Six: If you are responding to a state or federal RFP (Request for Proposals), follow the steps outlined in the application packet or on the Internet site. Public money (state or federal) has a specific format for application.

Step Seven: If you are seeking private money (foundations, corporations, charitable trusts) and you think you have a match, approach them with a simple *abstract* and *letter of intent.* Samples of both documents are included in Chapter Five (page 77). We have already discussed the abstract, and a letter of intent is a kind of cover letter, announcing your intention to submit a full proposal.

Step Eight: You may query, or approach, a few private funding sources at the same time. Some disagree with me on this point, but I say go ahead and send out two or three abstract/letter of intent packets and "see who bites." If you do get a bite, you can go ahead and work with them on developing a full proposal (narrative and budget).

Step Nine: Carefully proof and refine your abstract before submitting it for review. Ask several colleagues and someone outside of the "school world" or your agency to read the abstract. Remember, most private funding sources do not have boards made up of schoolteachers or social workers. Therefore, your written materials should make sense to anyone who picks them up to read and review.

Step Ten: Submit the abstract and letter of intent packet and hope for a green light or invitation to submit a full proposal. Then and only then do you write the full proposal, the complete narrative, and the budget. Moreover, if and when you are invited to submit a full proposal, the funding source will guide you in preparing the proposal in accordance with their expectations.

Remember, before you even think about writing a narrative or preparing a budget, do the research required for a "right match." This saves time, increases your chances for success, and improves the morale and confidence of the grant-writing team.

Question Two: What is the difference between public and private grant monies?

Grant dollars can come from two sources: *public money* or *private money.* Finding out where each kind of money can be found and how to approach each funding source is the topic of this section.

Public Money Grants

Public money refers to state or federal dollars. Here is your profile of public money.

What: State or federal funds that can be allotted in either competitive or designated awards. *Competitive awards* are those grants you or your group can apply for via a proposal. *Designated awards* indicate those grants that the state or federal government "bestows upon" a school or agency using some sort of per diem (per day) or per capita (by the head) formula.

Who: For public schools mostly, though private schools can get Eisenhower grant money for science and math curricula, and they may also qualify for other programs. It pays to check it out rather than just assume that you don't qualify because you represent a private or religious school.

When: These grants are awarded in cycles. Typically, a district or agency will seek a demonstration grant or "seed money" cycle of funding first to gather data or to test out a project. Then, with data in hand and a nod from the funding source, the district can apply for a full implementation cycle of funding.

Where: The best way to find out about federal money is on the Internet. Use your search engine to go to the site for the U.S. Department of Education. Then, go to the downlink for *grants and contracts.* It takes you to the Federal Register, where all grants, deadlines, guidelines, and other valuable information is posted. State money information is also available on the Internet, usually described on the state's home page. Often, this pot of money for schools or children's programs comes from a state lottery, bond, or luxury tax designated for that purpose. Sometimes, state money for teacher grants flows from a block grant (a large chunk of federal money handed down to a state) that comes out of Washington, DC. Again, to track block grants, use the Internet to visit the state's home page or the state department of education web site to hunt for grant postings. Or use your school's directory to the state department of education and find the name of the grant's coordinator. This individual can keep you up to date on state grant funds.

How: Federal or state grants are typically big grants ($25,000 or more) and are awarded to facilitate large or multi-year projects. These grants are often demanding and difficult to write and may require *matching funds, in-kind funds,* and *significant research.*

Key Words: These words are important in writing a public-money grant: *systemic change, national standards, Goals 2000, free* and *reduced lunch rate, standardized test data,* and *under-represented populations.*

Key Idea: With public-money grants, your key idea is to "sound pitiful." Emphasize the pitiful test scores in your school and you will get the attention of the funding source. In contrast, private-money grants fund "prestigious ideas." Read on to find out more.

Private Money Grants

Who: Both private schools and public schools can apply for these dollars, though you will probably need to have a 501-c-3 letter, an IRS tax document that says your institution is both tax exempt and nonprofit, in order to apply. Also, check the "limitations" section in the guidelines for each group that you approach. Private funding sources typically limit their favors to a select group that shares their goals or that can benefit most from their resources.

What: Private money comes from private sources such as businesses, corporations, and families. Look for words such as *endowments, corporate giving, trusts, charitable trusts, funds,* and *foundations* to locate private money.

Why: Private donors set up foundations and trusts to give money for two reasons: (1) to get a tax break, and (2) to meet their agenda. Their agenda may be social, political, or simply to make the world a "better, safer, more healthy place."

When: Private money sources have either open cycles of funding, in which they accept letters of inquiry all year long, or some kind of spring/fall cycle, in which they accept letters of intent in the fall and notify you of funding in the spring.

Where: Look for private money sources in these places:

- On the Internet. Use your search engine to find *Grants, Teacher Grants,* or *Foundations.*

- By using resource books, such as *The Directory of Corporate Giving*, found in university or large public libraries. There are many expensive guides and directories of grant sources. Be careful, however, about buying them for yourself or your school. You can probably be quite productive by spending a few hours in a good library borrowing their reference books. These guides are found in the reference section of the library.

- Through professional journals and professional organizations, where Request for Proposals (RFP) are often posted.

- With the help of grant and funding newsletters. The phone numbers of three grant newsletters are included to your right. Call and ask for a sample copy before you order a subscription. Make sure that the newsletter meets your expectations.

How: Follow the guidelines in this chapter, page 14, on submitting an abstract and letter of intent. Private sources do not want to see a full proposal. They do not want phone calls. They want to review your idea via an abstract and letter of intent, and then *they call you.*

Key Words: These words are important in private-money grants: *corporate visibility, cutting-edge ideas, innovation, excellence, service,* and *high standards.*

Key Ideas: With private money, you want to "sound prestigious." These folks want to be associated with classy projects. Emphasize your innovation and how it will reflect positively on your funding source.

Remember, both private and public money sources can be approached if you do the research up front and make a good match.

Question Three: Does geography affect my funding chances?

Keep in mind the fact that private money sources often limit their awards to specific geographic areas. Some funding sources limit funding to cities or counties in which they have a plant, factory, or corporate office. Sometimes, private funding sources have an office in one state, but give money in another state. This may be because a board member has an important connection to that state. It is not unusual for a funding source to limit awards to one or two counties within a state. Don't be surprised to find that a large international company awards grants in just one or two cities or states.

Why are there geographic limitations? (1) It is their money. They can do what they want. (2) They want to limit the number of proposals they have to review. (3) The limitations may be there because the foundation has a personal reason for emphasizing gifts in that area, perhaps to honor someone from that city.

Carefully check out the geographic limitations information in the grant resource book or application packet. These limitations are real. They won't consider your proposal if you live outside of the region.

Question Four: Do I need a 501-c-3 letter?

You need a 501-c-3 letter if your school or agency wants to apply for most private money grants. A 501-c-3 letter is an official IRS (Internal Revenue Service) document that says that your group is both *tax exempt* and *non-profit*. A tax attorney must fill out and file this documentation. It is not free. Don't assume that your school or group already has a 501-c-3 letter. They may qualify for one but have never submitted the paperwork. If your public school district has a letter, then your school is covered.

You will know that you need this documentation because the grant application will say "limited to 501-c-3 organizations" or "attach a copy of your IRS tax number." Don't wait around for this letter. You need it before you apply for the grant. If you are not sure about the status or location of this document, ask the auditor for your school or agency.

Question Five: How does the choice of a topic affect my chances for funding?

What's hot and what's not? That discussion isn't limited to the fashion scene. It is relevant in the field of grant writing, too. State and federal funding sources like to initiate "cutting edge" ideas because it keeps the public happy. Private corporate funders enjoy the prestige that comes from being associated with a popular "model program." For a look at what I see as the "Top 10 Hot Topics for Grants," read on. For more good topics, classic topics that always seem fundable, check out *Grant Writing for Teachers* for "200 Hot Topics for Grants."

The Top 10 Hot Topics for Grants

1. **Abstinence-based Sex Education Programs:** With the illegitimacy rate edging past 90 percent in many urban centers, these programs are gaining credibility and urgency for funding. The focus is on mentoring boys and girls to make healthy choices to delay sexual activity until adulthood, preferably with marriage in mind. The boost comes from federal monies, which now carry a proviso that sex education programs must be abstinence-based in order to be funded.

2. **Character Education (Values Education):** School-wide initiatives to promote core values, such as work ethic, integrity, citizenship, and respect are popular. With the troubling increases in teen suicide and shootings, these programs are urgent funding considerations.

3. **Direct Instruction Programs:** These programs are popular for teacher-centered small groups, the whole class, or even one-on-one meetings as long as your project focuses on direct instruction with teachers in charge of children learning in measurable increments. Examples include programs like "Distar" and "Open Court" reading.

4. **Foreign Language Instruction:** These classes, especially in the early grades, are a hot topic. With new research

suggesting that the brain is "wired" to acquire a second language before the age of 10, new attention is being paid to projects that begin foreign language instruction formally and early.

5. **Internet Access:** The federal government is coming out with large block grants to put Internet access in every school. The key word here is not *access,* however. Good grants will be those that demonstrate the use of the Internet to support academic instruction.

6. **Mathematics:** Calculators, parent workshops, math resource rooms for schools—anything with math, except grants to buy randomly chosen piles of manipulatives, is fundable. The winners are those math grants that show a sequenced, developmentally appropriate instructional program for applied mathematics.

7. **Phonics:** Phonics is "fashionable" again. Programs, workbooks, videos, teacher training—anything to get children reading on grade level with a phonics emphasis is fundable.

8. **Science:** All science projects, especially physical and earth science, are fundable areas. Test scores have been dismal and that makes good fodder for the grant machine. Focus on one area of science in the curriculum and show how you will infuse national standards, such as *Benchmarks for Science Literacy,* into the new program or how your new resource center will enable teachers to fulfill state or local objectives for science.

9. **Service Learning Initiatives:** Teaching job skills, the work ethic, and hands-on applications of academics is popular. This also includes "tech prep" initiatives for which there is a wealth of federal funds.

10. **Special Education Grants:** With one in five youngsters receiving special education services in many districts, this is a critical area for funding. Preschool initiatives and "transition" grants to move students, at age 21, from school to a job or group home are popular.

Date _____

What Are Your Funding Ideas?

Directions: Brainstorm a few topics for upcoming grants. Do your ideas fit into one of the "Top 10 Hot Topics" in this chapter?

1. _____

_____

2. _____

_____

3. _____

_____

4. _____

_____

5. _____

_____

6. _____

_____

7. _____

_____

8. _____

_____

9. _____

_____

10. _____

_____

                   reproducible

Question Six: How do I match my need to buy materials with the funders' desire to try new ideas?

I always get worried when a potential grant writer introduces himself or herself to me with the words: "Dr. Bone, I want to buy . . . with my grant." You can fill in the blank with any number of important materials or new equipment. A few years ago, everyone wanted personal computers for classrooms. "Big books" and whole language materials were in demand. Recently, teachers have been asking for CD-ROM materials to supplement science and geography curricula and funds for field trips. Too bad they won't be *buying* anything unless they start *trying*—trying to implement change instead of stacking up purchases.

Your mantra in grant writing should be "I want to try", *not* "I want to buy." Grants are not rewards, gifts, or even incentives. Grants are opportunities to try innovations in teaching, to infuse creativity into instruction, and to "jump start" change efforts in communities. Grantors (those who give grants) want to be the ones who "make change happen" by funding those ideas that have the potential to make schools better, curricula more useful, and students more productive. So, if you really want to get your grant, focus on identifying a critical area of need and formulate an interesting or credible solution for meeting that need. Ignore the temptation to "throw money at a problem" by purchasing lots of pretty books or manipulatives, instead talk about how what you do will make a difference.

To get started, take a look at the "Fat Substitution Chart" for changing poor grant ideas into winning ideas. Think of this chart like the health magazine charts in which one substitutes fattening chips for slimming carrot sticks.

Fat Substitution Chart

Instead of Buying	Start Trying
Computers	Implementing a new technology plan
Juvenile Novels	Establishing a reading lab
Saltwater Aquariums	Integrating a school-wide study of marine life
CD-ROMs	Building a research strand into the science curriculum
Field Trips	Improving expressive language in young children by broadening their social experiences

26

Test Your Knowledge of Grant Sources

Directions: Make notes for further research about matching your idea to the appropriate grant source.

1. How will you identify the right private or public money source for your idea?

   _____

   _____

2. Does your organization have a 501-c-3 letter? What steps will you take to secure one?

   _____

   _____

3. Have you carefully reviewed the limitations to funding described in the grant application? Is geography an issue? Do your goals match those of the organization from which you are seeking a grant?

   _____

   _____

4. Explain the difference between sounding "pitiful" to get public money and "prestigious" to get private money.

   _____

   _____

5. Did you learn something new about newsletter or Internet sources for finding grant dollars? How will you apply that knowledge?

   _____

   _____

Date _____

Practice Switching from "Buy" to "Try"

Directions: Write a few sentences about what you want to *buy* with your grant.

_____

_____

_____

_____

Now, reframe your thinking in terms of the curriculum or programming changes you want to *try* with your grant.

_____

_____

_____

_____

What differences do you see?

_____

_____

_____

_____

_____

Chapter Three: Solving Problems of Narrative Design

Once you have cleared the critical hurdle of finding the right funding source for your proposal, it is time to begin the work of designing and writing the narrative. Every grant has two parts—the *narrative* and the *budget.*

Whether you are writing a two-page "mini-grant" for the PTA or a 20-page fine arts grant proposal for the National Endowment for the Arts, the grant will comprise some kind of narrative and a budget.

In the narrative, you tell your story. In the budget, you explain the cost of the project and how the cost will be covered. In *Grant Writing for Teachers,* I describe the steps in preparing each phase of the six-part narrative. This book, however, offers a more intense, advanced discussion of how to avoid specific problems in narrative design.

The Major Parts of a Grant Narrative and Their Functions

Project Summary or Description: Introduces the title, topic, and purpose of your proposal.

Justification or Needs Statement: Gives a rationale for funding the project; includes research and letters of support.

Goals and Objectives: Outlines the expectations for the project.

Procedures or Activities: Gives examples of how the expectations will be fulfilled; tells specifically how you will accomplish the project.

Evaluation Criteria: Explains the measures you will take to assess the success of the project's objectives.

Dissemination Plan: Describes the methods you will use to extend the project to other schools or share your message with the community.

Addenda: Attachments to the narrative that explain, justify, extend, support, or give information.

The 10 Most Common Problems in Narrative

1. There is too much jargon or a wordy, loose use of language throughout the narrative. Avoid rambling on about "how much you need this project."

2. No catchy title for the project.

3. The objectives and evaluation criteria do not match.

4. The evaluation criteria are weak and there are no examples, such as pre-tests or surveys, to show how you will measure success.

5. Poor justification. No test scores, surveys, research, or letters of support to offer credibility.

6. Confusion between procedures and activities. Procedures are step-by-step descriptions of how the project will unfold, while activities should be examples of what children or students will do as part of the project.

7. The narrative presentation is sloppy. Examples include typographical errors, correction fluid, spelling errors, poorly reproduced attachments, or text smaller than 12-point font.

8. The guidelines are not followed. If "they" say that there is a 10-page, double-spaced limit on narrative, then "they" mean it!

9. A careless dissemination plan. When people give you money, they want plenty of press and publicity.

10. Too much text. Use outlines, bullets, boxes, graphs, and figures to break up the text and make the proposal easy on the eyes.

In the following sections, you will find detailed solutions and pragmatic suggestions for fixing the top 10 problems in narrative design. There are not 10 different sections because many of the problems coexist. For example, the justification issue is closely related to the evaluation issue, so read both sections in order to get all the information you need.

How to Create a Title That Tantalizes the Reader

One of the weaknesses in narrative is the lack of an exciting title. The title should be introduced to the reader in the project description or summary and should be underlined, bold-faced, or italicized throughout the narrative. Read on to find out how titles can strengthen your narrative and how you can create winning titles.

A True Story

I was sitting with a novice teacher, helping her to design a $2,000 mini-grant that would help her to improve literacy at the small, rural school where she was completing her first year of teaching. Our conversation went something like this:

"So, you want to improve literacy . . . what do you mean by that?" I asked.

"Literacy. Well, I want the children to read more. They don't read much at home," the young teacher replied.

"Why is that?" I prompted.

"Lots of reasons. Their parents are poor, you know. They (i.e., families) don't even get a daily newspaper. Some families don't have telephones out in isolated parts of the county. So, the children don't have books in their homes."

"We could add a field trip to the grant budget for the children to get their own library cards. That way they could ask their parents to stop at the county library when they come into town," I offered.

"Yes. That's good. But what about my Family Reading Workshop?" she continued.

"You want to use $500 for a reading workshop when so few parents even come into school for meetings or PTA? Why do you think they would come in for a night to learn about reading to children?" I quizzed.

"I thought I had to have a workshop," the young teacher replied. "Isn't that what I should do?"

"Maybe not," I said. "Do something different. Something that would really meet the needs of these families . . . these rural families."

Then it hit me. The perfect title for the grant, and suddenly the ideas began to flow. Our conversation continued.

"I've got it . . . *Rural Route Literacy!*" I exclaimed.

"What?" my protégé wondered.

"That's the perfect title for your grant—*Rural Route Literacy*. We will use that $500 to give subscriptions of high-quality children's magazines to each family in your kindergarten class."

The young teacher caught on. "And the magazines will be delivered to those rural mailboxes at each home."

"And the parents can see the children getting excited about receiving their own magazines," I added.

"And younger siblings can read the magazines, too, or just look at the pictures. And you know, Dr. Bone, the parents won't have to drive to the school for a night meeting that they won't really enjoy. Those magazines continue all year long!" she finished.

All this creative energy was released when we stumbled on a "title that tantalizes" (see What Makes a Tantalizing Title?, page 34).

Why a Title Works for Your Grant

I have assisted writers in writing over $2 million worth of grants, maybe much more. In every case, a strong title has helped the writers to create a cohesive narrative, develop innovative activities, design appropriate evaluation tools, and justify a fair budget.

All this from a good title? You bet. The title simply "pulls it all together," for you, the writer, and for the grant readers. In fact, your title is so important that I tell writers to bold face, italicize, and/or underline the title throughout the narrative.

- *A Pleasing Sound*

- *A Clear Message About Your Grant*

- *Personalized*

- *Exciting*

- *Rich in Information*

- *Credible*

Five Ways to Develop a Tantalizing Title

1. Alliteration Is Attractive

Phonics Is Fashionable—a first-grade reading program

Inquiry, Investigation, and Information—a middle-grade science center

Marvelous Middle-Grade Math—a math manipulative grant

2. Acronyms Can Work if They Aren't Too Cute or Confusing

Project BOWS: Biographies of Women Scientists—a girls/science grant for the high school media center

Project IF: Investigation Fundamentals—a chemistry lab grant for middle school

Project GOLD: Girls Organizing, Leading, Deciding—a mentoring and decision-making program for at-risk girls

3. Metaphor Titles: A Message and Meaning Title

Rural Route Literacy—sending children's magazines to rural homes

Caring for Kids—a latch-key kids program

Wise Buys—an economics course for sixth graders

4. Clue into the Curriculum

Geo-Centered Learning—setting up six geography centers that meet the National Geography Standards

Service Learning for Sixth Graders—teaching sixth graders the value of work and the work ethic

Character Chats—a character education grant to be implemented school-wide in a primary school

5. Bandwagon Titles

Let's Go GEO!—you've got it, a geography grant

Write On!—right on the mark, a writing center for third grade

Super Science!—more science centers

As you read these titles, can't you just imagine the grants unfolding? The title pulls your grant together, and as you infuse the title into the narrative, it pulls the reader along, too. For more ideas on creating titles, see pages 44–46 of *Grant Writing for Teachers*.

Remember, use the title throughout your narrative. Instead of beginning a paragraph with *This proposal . . .* , say Rural Route Literacy *will . . .* , and you will keep readers interested.

How to Write Effective Goals and Objectives

By the time you get to goals and objectives in your grant proposal, you might be tempted to relax. After all, writing the justification section (covered on pages 39–41) and finding creative titles and themes seem to be more demanding tasks. But don't make that mistake. Your goals and objectives will be carefully scrutinized by grant readers. No amount of creativity, innovation, or glaring need can compensate for poorly written objectives or overly ambitious goal statements. The goals and objectives of your grant are the infrastructure of the document. Think of steel girders for a skyscraper. The lines must be lean, strong, and galvanized or the structure will topple.

If you need to review more detailed guidelines for writing these statements, refer to *Grant Writing for Teachers*. Chapter Six is devoted to the art of designing goals and objectives that will strengthen your proposal.

Here is a review of goal design:

- A goal is a broad statement about what the project will accomplish.

- A goal is not the same as a specific, measurable objective.

- "Less is more" in goal setting. A few, well-thought-out goals go a long way in adding credibility to your proposal.

- Avoid jargon and loose, rambling statements in goals.

Here is an example of a poorly written goal and then a rewritten version:

Original. The goal of this project is to help all children recognize their potential for mathematical excellence so that they can be productive citizens in the new millennium.

Rewrite. The goal of *Math Buddies* is to improve math computation scores among third-grade students at Happy Days Elementary School by providing a math tutoring program two days per week.

Do you see the differences between the two goal statements?

Write your observations here and then practice rewriting the goals that follow.

_____

_____

_____

_____

Now practice on these syrupy, overwrought goals.

Original. The goal of this grant is to keep all children safe from harm while their parents struggle to make a living in the year 2000.

Rewrite:

_____

_____

_____

_____

Original. The goal of this project is to make the arts come alive for every child in the town of Hillville so that he or she has access to the beauty of music and drama.

Rewrite:

_____

_____

_____

_____

Do you see how goal statements carry the title and the message of your grant? It is a good idea to have one or two goals for your grant, and more objectives. Too many goal statements make your proposal seem unattainable. Set goals that make sense. Don't try to dazzle your reader. Convince him or her that you know what could _really happen_ if you get the grant.

Remember our proverb about the building of sand falling? Each section of your proposal gains strength, or becomes weaker, as sections are added.

A New Look at Objectives

Moving on to objectives, one should use one of the following formats:

1. Students will be able to . . .

2. By the end of the project year (   ) students will . . .

3. Participants will have the opportunity to . . .

4. By engaging in Project (   ), participants will . . .

Fill in the rest of the sentence with a _measurable verb._ Be specific. Give numbers, dates, and data.

For example:

1. Students will be able to *visit six sites to engage in mentoring projects.*

2. By the end of the project year 2000, students will *complete four strands of pre-algebra curriculum with an average score of 80 percent or better in each strand.*

3. Participants will have the opportunity to *read three books every nine weeks, which correlates to district science objectives.*

4. By engaging in Project LOVE, *participants from the Sunny Side Housing Development will develop positive parenting skills through attending weekly parenting support groups coordinated through Sunny Side Primary School.*

Remember that in grant writing, "less is more." Design enough objectives to support the work that will be accomplished with the grant. However, be careful to show how your objectives match up with your budget. For example:

Sample One: Students will write three original books during each nine-week period. It looks okay, right? Wrong. How does the grant reader know that you need many dollars to accomplish this objective? Don't all good teachers involve students in writing? What's new about this?

Sample Two: Students will write three original books during each nine-week period, by working with the "Let's Write" software program and using the ink-jet printer and other materials in the Sunny Side Primary Publishing Center.

Do you get it? The software, printer, and other materials are available because you bought them with grant funds! The objective won't happen unless the Sunny Side Primary Publishing Center happens!

The next step—matching objectives with evaluation statements that make sense. We'll discuss the design of appropriate, matching evaluation criteria later in this chapter.

How to Make the Justification Persuasive and Sound

Justification, *needs statement, statement of need,* or *rationale*—these are all terms for the portion of your narrative statement in which you must explain why this proposal is necessary. A weak justification of the project is one of the 10 most common problems in grant writing; and in my opinion, the one that requires the most skill to remedy.

This may sound harsh, but so be it. If you don't know what you are talking about, then it will show up in this part of the narrative. If you are not familiar with the research in your field, if you haven't checked your facts and data, if you don't know the population that you're working with, it shows up here and your proposal is doomed. How do you make the justification section work for you, not against you? Read on.

A Discussion About Justification

I love that old jazz tune that says "It don't mean a thing if it ain't got that swing." This segment of grant writing, the need for a strong justification for funding your project, shows you how to convince the reader that your program is worthy of both recognition and dollars.

Does your justification "have that swing"? Does the narrative convince, prove, substantiate, justify, dignify, qualify, and support your goals and objectives? Your task is to "swing" the reader over to your side. Carefully controlled wording, aligned in four critical sections, will help you to design a strong justification section.

In *Grant Writing for Teachers,* I devote an entire chapter to justification. There are checklists, phrases, tactics, and ideas to help you plan and write this portion of your narrative. But for now, focus on the fact that a successful justification section must accomplish 10 persuasive tasks:

1. Explain the rationale for your proposal.

2. State the reasons why your proposal is important.

3. Convince readers of the importance and impact of the grant you are preparing.

4. Justify your request for funds.

5. Defend your proposal's value.

6. Confirm the need for a program like the one you propose.

7. Present data/studies that uphold the need for your project.

8. Affirm your project by presenting letters of support.

9. Legitimize your proposal by linking it to current research.

10. Seek approval for your project by defining critical needs and substantial problem areas.

To accomplish these daunting tasks, your justification section should be organized around four sections:

1. **Describe the client group.** Tell them who you are serving. Give specific numbers of children, classes, and teachers who will be involved. Offer a clear and persuasive discussion of the setting and scope of the problem that this client group or school is experiencing.

2. **Present both qualitative (ethnographic) and quantitative (statistical) data that supports the need for your program or proposed idea.** A nice mix of test scores, surveys, case studies, anecdotes, and attitude inventories is the best choice.

3. **Link your proposal to current research.** Cite timely studies that illustrate the problem you address, and/or share studies that showcase a program similar to yours that was successful. If addenda are permitted, attach copies of articles, highlighting important data and quotes with a yellow or orange marker.

4. **Strengthen your case with expert support.** The letter of support adds credibility to your proposal. Secure one or more letters from "experts," such as university faculty, professionals, authors, researchers, or parents, who describe both the need for your program and their personal support

for the project. In cases in which you are asking for "matching funds," the CEO or administrator should cite a dollar amount that the organization will offer to support the project.

Justification could easily become a weak link in your proposal. It is too easy to rely on purely anecdotal evidence or personal opinions and neglect the "real meat." Remember, "It don't mean a thing if it ain't got that swing." Can your justification section "swing" the opinion of the reader?

Date _____

Test Your Justification Skills

Directions: After reading the preceding section, make a list of ways that you can strengthen the justification section of a previously rejected grant, or build a strong justification section for a grant on which you are currently working.

1. Do I have the four parts of justification carefully outlined?

_____

Changes to make:

_____

_____

_____

2. Have I attached attractive, clear addenda to support the need for my project?

_____

Changes to make:

_____

_____

_____

3. Is my research strong and up to date? Have I used tables, bullets, or graphs to make the research easy to access?

_____

Changes to make:

_____

_____

_____

4. Have I secured letters of support that are typed on official stationery and that contain specific references to my organization and the title of the grant? Can I find someone whose credentials or title will "pull weight" with the readers?

_____

Changes to make:

_____

_____

_____

5. Have I used clear, persuasive language and avoided jargon?

_____

Changes to make:

_____

_____

_____

- *Did you meet the goals that were set?*

- *To what degree were you successful in meeting the goals and objectives?*

- *How did you support objectives that document the outcomes of the project?*

- *How did you present the data that illustrates the outcomes of the project?*

How to Design Effective Evaluation Criteria That Match the Objectives

During the past few years, I have learned a few lessons about what makes a grant go all the way to approval. We have discussed several positive aspects of grant writing in previous sections of Chapter Three: strong titles, winning topics, and strong justification. This section focuses on negative, sloppy evaluation criteria.

Looking at grant proposal after grant proposal and talking with other grant readers leads me to believe that sloppy evaluation criteria tables your grant faster than almost anything else. If the evaluation is weak, readers take a second, harder look at the rest of your narrative. The idea seems to be—*If the evaluation is sloppy, then the proposal is weak.*

Weak evaluation dilutes the impact of the entire proposal. Many times, teachers are surprised when their evaluation criteria are found to be lacking. They say, "I thought it was adequate." Apparently not. Take a look at the sidebar to your left, to see what your evaluation criteria must satisfy.

In Chapter Seven of *Grant Writing for Teachers*, I share specific methods for designing excellent evaluations for your grant. These methods, along with examples of both strong and weak evaluation criteria may help you to avoid the pitfalls of evaluation.

As you create your evaluation criteria, remember the Golden Rule of writing narrative—*If you create a test or document to show need, use that same test or document as an evaluation tool.* Here's how it works. Let's say that you are writing a grant to purchase classroom maps, globes, and materials to teach geography in creative ways. To show need, design a pre-post test called *Mrs. Jones' Geography Quiz.* This teacher-made assessment documents your students' pitiful performance in world geography and validates your need to purchase $2,500 worth of materials, books, and speakers to boost geography scores.

Hint: Use that same instrument as an evaluation tool. Attach the test as an addendum to the proposal. That's a winning and productive use of evaluation tools!

Now, let's practice making a match between an objective and an evaluation criterion. I'll do the first one for you, and then you try your hand at it.

Objective One: Students will improve their skills in mechanics of language by participating in *Project WRITE.*

Evaluation One: Teachers will informally check student writing to note improvement in spelling and grammar. (Poor Evaluation)

Evaluation One (revised): By the end of the project year 1999–2000, students participating in *Project WRITE* will demonstrate an increase of one to three percentage points on the state writing skills test in the area of mechanics of language. (Better Evaluation)

Evaluation One (revised): By the end of the project year 1999–2000, students participating in Project WRITE will demonstrate improvement in spelling and grammar skills by having three writing tasks evaluated by their teacher each nine weeks. The attached writing rubric will be used to assess students' writing. (Better Evaluation)

Both of the "better" evaluations work. You might prefer more traditional standardized test data to the authentic use of rubrics, or you might want to include both kinds of proof.

Note that the "rubric" would be attached as an addendum, so that the grant readers could examine your method of documentation. You would have the option of using a rubric or checklist that you made up, or selecting one from another source. For example, many grant-writing teachers like to use instruments from my three Good Apple assessment books:

- *Primarily Portfolios* (1995) Early Childhood Level
- *Authentic Instruction and Assessment* (1995) Elementary Level
- *Middle Grade Assessment* (1998) Middle School Level

Each of these resource books contains a broad span of generic, reproducible assessment tools that can be attached as addenda to the evaluation section of your narrative.

Date _____

Test Your Evaluation Design Skills

1. Write an objective for a grant on which you are currently working or one that was rejected.

   Objective One:

   _____

   _____

2. Design two different evaluation criteria that would match this objective.

   Evaluation One (traditional):

   _____

   _____

   Evaluation One (authentic):

   _____

   _____

3. What did you learn about the use of addenda to support evaluation criteria?

   _____

   _____

4. List some techniques that you plan to use in your next grant to make the evaluation section stronger.

   _____

   _____

How to Make a Powerful Dissemination Plan

Duuring my seminars on *Grant Writing for Teachers,* the term *dissemination* always confuses a large number of teachers.

"Is it a marketing term?" asked one educator.

"Does it have to do with training?" inquired another.

"It sounds like it has something to do with reproduction, not grant writing," laughed one honest soul.

To an extent, they were all correct! Dissemination is a fairly brief, yet critical part of the narrative or written portion of the grant proposal. This is a part of the proposal that readers discern carefully and decide whether you have followed through with important objectives and target ideas expressed in earlier portions of the narrative.

Dissemination means to "share the news." Your job is to convince the reader of three things:

1. You will reach an important and appropriate audience and tell them about your project. This could be other teachers and administrators, or may also include parents and students. Think of this as a staff development component of the grant.

2. You will give credit to the funding source, be it a philanthropic group or a government agency. Everybody wants to look good and feel appreciated. In this sense, your audience is the wider community at large. Think of this as a public relations plan for the grant.

3. You will spread your "model," "idea," or "method" as far and wide as you can. If possible, you will create the opportunity for others to try your idea in their own schools. Think of this as a marketing plan for your product or idea.

In sum, dissemination can be part staff development—part public relations and part marketing plan. That is a lot of ground to cover for a narrative that could be as short as half a page in length! Remember, when designing your dissemination plan, follow two crucial steps:

- **Read the project guidelines carefully.** Respond to the funder's interests in dissemination. For example, I often find that private money sources are seeking good public relations. They want to be recognized! On the other hand, government funding sources are more often concerned with training teachers to take the ball and run with it. Public money sources want model programs to be disseminated around the state or nation.

- **Create a memorable, yet workable plan that gets the reader's attention.** How can you formulate a unique, yet practical dissemination plan or strategy?

Dissemination Plans

- A web page on the Internet (this can be generated by students)

- Presentations at professional conferences and workshops (by teachers)

- Brochures and newsletters

- Media coverage, such as interviews on television and radio

- Logos on book bags and backpacks

- Traditional conferences to disseminate research

- Publications in journals and magazines

- Be specific and match the dissemination plan to both the objectives and time-line portions of the narrative. There should be a neat connection between these sections. For example, if you plan to present your idea at the state math educator's conference as part of the dissemination plan, then your target date for that presentation should be included on the time line.

Dissemination can be exciting to design. It is your chance to sit back at the end of the proposal and say, "Now here's what we did!" Your level of commitment to the project and to its ideals can be felt through the dissemination plan, so don't let your momentum lag.

In the next section, we will discuss common problems encountered in going after technology dollars and the "Ethics of Grant Writing." Before we move on, let's apply what you have learned about dissemination.

Date _____

Dissemination Dreams

Directions: Dream up some creative dissemination ideas for your proposal. Write your ideas below and apply them to the next grant you write.

Other Common Problems in Narrative

Tackling Technology Grants

In going after technology money (grants for computers, software, Internet access, and other forms of electronic learning), educators should be aware of several common errors that weaken one's chances for funding.

- **The absence of a five-year technology plan attached as an addendum to the proposal.** Funders want to see how your school or agency already uses technology before they give you any more.

- **An inflated budget.** Don't expect to get a whole lab or computers for every classroom from one grant. Ask for a few things and explain how you will use them.

- **A missing staff development plan.** Make sure that you include a time line for staff development, a written plan for staff development, and a budget for staff development. Nobody wants to give grant money to a group that has no plan to train the people who will use the technology. For an excellent explanation of this critical issue, read the article "The Computer Delusion" found in the July 1997 issue of *The Atlantic Monthly* magazine. The author, Todd Oppenheimer, describes how computers and other technology do not seem to significantly improve learning because of our poor use of the technology and a lack of appropriate, supportive staff development.

- **The technology is not "infused with instruction."** You should not ask for technology money unless you plan to use the technology to meet learning objectives in all subject areas. Internet access and PCs are expensive, distracting toys in the classroom and funders are taking a hard look at *how*

you will use the technology to meet objectives. These kinds of descriptions would be found in the procedures and activities section of the narrative.

• A term I use, *letting your slip show,* is when the reader can tell that you don't know what you are talking about with technology and that there is no strong technology person on staff. If you don't understand the use of the technology you are asking for in the grant, then hire a consultant to help you write the proposal.

Notes on Technology Grants: What Have You Learned?

_____

_____

_____

_____

_____

_____

_____

_____

_____

_____

_____

_____

_____

_____

Other Common Problems: Time Lines

Many grant proposals ask for a time line (schedule) for the project. The time line should be succinct, visually appealing, and contain all pertinent dates in the implementation, evaluation, and dissemination of the project. Here are some common mistakes in time-line design.

- **Leaving out evaluation dates.** For example, if you are going to use the MAT-7 standardized test as evaluation, then list the next test date on the time line.

- **Putting too much information on the time line.** Don't rehash the narrative. Just put *March 2000, MAT-7 Testing* for evaluation.

- **Neglecting to frame a plan on the time line.** Don't just put *September to May: Implementation* of the project. Try to impose some sort of plan so that the readers see your organization. Try this:

September–October 2000	Physical science units (magnets, electricity)
October 2000	Post-test on physical science
October 2000	Field trip to power plant
November–December 2000	Earth science units (weather, oceanography)
December 2000	Post-test on earth science
December 2000	Field trip to weather station
January–March 2001	Life science units (plants, animals)
March 2001	Post-test on life science
March 2001	Field trip to zoo
April–May 2001	Environmental science units
May 2001	School science fair
May 2001	Post-test and state science tests

Can you tell that this is a time line for an elementary school science grant? If you can, then the time line is effective.

Other Common Problems: The Ethics of Grant Writing

Grant writing is a step forward in one's professional development, whether in teaching, administration, public service, or children's programming. One moves from simply implementing what others tell you to do to deciding what should be done by setting up new programs that require grant money. As in any new professional growth, there may be some hard lessons to learn and some surprises. I find it important to discuss the ethics of grant writing before one runs into a problem. Here are some rules to follow.

- Do not copy another teacher's grant without his or her written permission. That includes the sample grants in Chapter Five. They are there to give you guidance and ideas only!

- Always inform your administrator or board when you begin the process of seeking a grant. It is not only polite; it is required.

- Be aware of the mission statement of the foundation from which you are seeking funding. Do they promote the same kinds of curricula and beliefs that your school or agency holds dear? For an excellent discussion of this issue, read Nicholas Lemann's "Citizen 501-c-3" in the February 1997 issue of *The Atlantic Monthly*.

- Be truthful and frugal with budgets and funds. If you asked for $500 for science materials, don't spend that money on field trips. If you need to make a budget change, then go through the appropriate procedure for amending the budget.

- Put the needs of the children you are working for above your personal agenda, but don't compromise your values either.

Date _____

Wrapping Up Chapter Three

I could go on and on about the glitches and foul-ups that I have seen in grants prepared by teachers and others who work with children. Sometimes, the mistakes are more serious and cost the grant writer his or her shot at funding. Before we move into Chapter Four, where you will find some exciting new sources for funding your grant ideas, take some time to jot down your thoughts about the following:

Ethics in Grant Writing:

_____

_____

_____

Time Lines:

_____

_____

_____

Technology Grants:

_____

_____

_____

Grant Organization and Narrative:

_____

_____

_____

Date _____

What Have You Learned?

Directions: Circle **T** for true or **F** for false.

1. Successful grant writers seem to demonstrate a number of common attributes, attitudes, and actions. **T   F**

2. Private money and public money are not the same kind of money. **T   F**

3. Dissemination can be part public relations and part staff development. **T   F**

4. It is not ethical to "borrow" a grant from another source without permission. **T   F**

5. Time lines should use visual aids and succinct text. **T   F**

6. If the funding source sets a limit on the number of pages in the narrative or for addenda (attachments), it means it. **T   F**

7. Sloppy presentation is one of the top 10 mistakes made in grant writing. **T   F**

8. The Internet is the best place to find out what's going on with federal grants. **T   F**

9. It is a good idea to ask for a sample copy of a grant resource newsletter before you order a subscription. **T   F**

10. Justification has four parts and research is a critical one. **T   F**

11. Letters of support can be helpful, especially if you get one from an expert who has an important title or who is recognized. **T   F**

12 Lack of a staff development plan can blow the fuse on a technology grant. **T   F**

Review

All of the answers are true for Worksheet 10. How well did you do? If you need to review, go back to the following:

1. Chapter One: The entire chapter (page 3)

2. Chapter Two: Private vs. Public Money (page 18)

3. Chapter Three: Dissemination (page 47)

4. Chapter Three: Ethics of Grant Writing (page 54)

5. Chapter Three: Time Lines (page 53)

6. Chapter Three: 10 Most Common Problems (page 31)

7. Chapter Three: 10 Most Common Problems (page 31)

8. Chapter Two: Private vs. Public Money (page 18)

9. Chapter Two: Three Newsletters to Review (page 21)

10. Chapter Three: How to Make the Justification Section Persuasive and Sound (page 39)

11. Chapter Three—How to Make the Justification Section Persuasive and Sound (page 39)

12. Chapter Three: Tackling Technology Grants (page 51)

Now, we move into Chapter Four, where you will find sources for grants, both private and public money sources.

Chapter Four:
Where's the Money?

Our words of wisdom for Chapter Four come from an Indian language: "Many drops make a great flood." This particular adage meshes perfectly with my philosophy of finding grant dollars. I have never been one to hunt persistently for the perfect grant. Instead, I gather many interesting, provocative, smaller grants and use them to meet very specific needs or interests. I liken this approach to grant finding to my personal vegetarian eating habits. I don't eat large meals with a hunk of meat in the center of the plate; instead, I prefer smaller, nutritious snacks of grains and veggies that keep me going.

Of course, there is a place for a "big meal" in every diet. You, too, will feast on a big grant one day. However, it should be later, rather than sooner. Read the section on "Following the Hierarchy of Grants," beginning on page 74.

Also in this chapter you will find a directory of "51 Sources for Schools and Nonprofit Groups." There are both private and public money sources, and funders for small, large, and even mini-grants for novice writers.

Before you begin reviewing the 51 sources, take a look at some general guidelines and warnings for using books and resources that explain where one can find grant money.

Alternative Ways to Look for Grant Money

There are plenty of good places to find out about grant money. However, you should understand that grants and fund-raising are an industry unto themselves, and that people are out to make money from your need to find money for schools and community groups. If you bought this book, then you have already spent money on the search for grants. However, this book only costs a few dollars. Many of the resources for grant writers cost hundreds of dollars and may not give you what you expect. Be very discerning about ordering books or CD-ROMs with grant sources on them until you are certain what is included. Here are some alternatives I have seen schools use to avoid overspending on grant books.

- Use the resources in a local college or public library.

- Buy a few grant books and keep them in a central location for teachers around the district to use.

- Form a consortium with several smaller districts and set up a "grant center" that houses books and newsletters and hosts workshops with grant consultants.

- Bring in a grant-writing consultant to do staff development for teachers.

- Subscribe to a few grant newsletters and have a lead teacher in the school disseminate the information.

Popular Resources for Grant Writers

- Education Grants Alert weekly newsletter, 1-800-655-5597
- Foundation and Corporate Grants Alert, 1-800-655-5597
- Grants for School Districts newsletter, (617) 542-0048
- Funding Alert newsletter, (803) 750-9759
- *The Directory of Corporate and Foundation Givers** (available in many universities or public libraries)
- The Foundation Center Online Library, http://fdncenter.org/onlib/
- *The Foundation Directory** (available from the Foundation Center), 1-800-424-9836
- *Grant Writing for Teachers* (Good Apple, 1994), 1-800-421-5565
- Fund-raising Software, Blackbaud, Inc., 1-800-443-9441
- *The Chronicle of Philanthropy,* http://www.philanthropy.com/
- *Electronic Learning Magazine,* http://www.scholastic.com/el/index.htm
- *Teaching K–8**,* http://www.teachingk-8.com/
- *The Good Apple Newspaper,* 1-800-421-5565
- Education Week Online**, http://www.edweek.org

*These periodicals offer a "grants alert" or articles on grant writing in each issue.

**Search the archives using the term *grants* for more information.

Unexpected Places to Find Grant Money

Grant resource books, newsletters, and the Internet are all excellent places to find grant dollars, but there are a few more unexpected free places to find mini-grants and awards that are perfect for novice or busy grant writers.

Professional Organizations. There are two reasons why joining a professional organization helps you find grant dollars. First, the journals, or newsletters, of the organizations typically publish RFPs (grant notices) as a service. Second, many organizations give grants themselves, and only their members may apply. There is a third, more subtle reason to stay involved in professional organizations. Many times, your resume or vita is required as part of the grant package, because the grantors want to know about the educators with whom they might be working. When the grantors see that you are professionally connected, your credibility and fundability increase!

Teaching Magazines. Magazines such as *The Good Apple Newspaper, Teaching K–8, Instructor,* and *Electronic Learning* often publish grants alert notices and regular columns on grant-writing techniques that include grant sources. For example, I have been writing *The Good Apple Newspaper* column, "Grant Writing: The Road to Riches," for three years. *Electronic Learning,* which is a free publication, also features an excellent grant-writing column. (Note that the *Electronic Learning* magazine is now part of *Instructor* magazine. However, you can check out the archives of *Electronic Learning* magazine on the Internet at: www.scholastic.com/inschool/. Internet addresses are quite fickle, so keep in mind that *Electronic Learning* can be found at the *Scholastic* magazine home page.

Newsletters from Corporations and Banks. I was sitting in an airport, waiting for my flight to Charlotte, North Carolina, when I noticed a friendly lady reading her company's newsletter. The cover story was "Community Grants a Great Success." Of course, I introduced myself as a "grant hound" and asked for her

newsletter when she was finished. I have found a number of state and local grants for teachers in company newsletters, church bulletins, and newspaper articles. This is sort of a "reverse osmosis" technique for finding grant money. In the newsletter or newspaper account, you typically read about grants that have already been funded. That's okay, because you can go ahead and call for an application for the next cycle of funding. Of course, you add the clipping or newsletter to your grant file or notebook!

Conferences and Workshops. Often, state and federal grants are first announced at professional workshops and conferences. For example, last spring at a teacher-education workshop, the keynote speaker from Washington announced an interesting new grant opportunity, and our group was the first to hear of it.

Networking with Other Educators. One of the best methods for finding out about grants is the same method you use to find out about good jobs, good restaurants, and good pediatricians—friends and colleagues. Talk informally with teachers who are "grant friendly," or try something more formal—a graduate class on grant writing. When I offer the "Grant Writing for Teachers" course for graduate credit, 30 percent of the student's grade is based on the development of a grant notebook. Each teacher in the course must find 10 private money sources and five public money sources for grant money, and they cannot be the same as anyone else's. Of course, on the last day of the course, we do a big swap, and every teacher ends up with a bulging notebook of grant sources!

Date _____

How Many New Funding Sources Can You Name?

Which new funding sources interest you? Write your plans for investigating new sources below.

_____

_____

_____

_____

_____

_____

_____

_____

_____

_____

_____

_____

_____

_____

_____

_____

_____

_____

Using the Internet

The Internet is probably the fastest, most up-to-date method for finding grant dollars. I recommend using the Internet in three ways:

Check Periodically. Periodically, I visit my favorite grant sites on the web and check out what's new in grants. Some of those favorites are listed at the end of this section. I print out new information or grant applications and put them in a three-ring binder.

Use Search Engines. About every three months, I spend an hour doing a search using Yahoo!™ or Infoseek™ (search engines) to explore new sites for grant information. I use key words such as *grants, education grants, grants for teachers,* or *charitable giving.* In every search, something new and helpful turns up. I print out what I want and put it in my grant notebook and "bookmark" the site as a favorite.

Check Corporate Sources. Finally, I use the Internet to track down grants that companies give. Most major corporations, such as General Electric, Toyota, and Exxon have funds used for education and community grants. I visit their home pages, down-link to the foundation or grants site, and e-mail a request for the annual report, grants application, or information packet on the foundation.

Internet Sites

Here are some of my favorite Internet sites for grants. I have listed only a few, because web addresses are subject to change. Once you visit the sites, however, you will get a feel for using the Internet as a grant resource.

Yahoo!™ Education Grants Link
http://search.yahoo.com/search?p=education+grants

U.S. Department of Education Grants and Contracts
http://gcs.ed.gov

Infoseek™ Grants Link
http://infoseek.go.com/Titles?qt=grants

Chalkboard
http://thechalkboard.com/

Grant Resources for Educators
http://www.leeric.lsu.edu/index3.htm

U.S. Department of Education (ED)—Funding
http://www.ed.gov/funding.html

http://www.ed.gov/Technology/

National Science Foundation
http://www.nsf.gov/home/grants.htm

Philanthropy News Network
http://pj.org

51 Sources for Schools and Nonprofit Groups

Here's what you've been waiting for—51 sources for education grants, in alphabetical order. To proceed, call, e-mail, write, or fax for an application packet. The application packet will give you the information you need to find out if this source is a good match for you. Review Chapter Two (page 13) for more information on making a good match.

1. **A+ for Kids Teacher Network Awards**
   Visit their web site at:
   http://www.netstage.com/apluskid/toc.html
   $300 mini-grants for model programs to share with other teachers

2. **American Association of University Women (AAUW)**
   (319) 337-1716
   $500–$1,500 grants for programs for young women

3. **American Chemical Society**
   (202) 872-6366
   Science awards of $100 to $1,000

4. **American Honda Foundation**
   (310) 781-4090
   Math and science grants, $40,000 to $80,000 annually

5. **American Teacher Awards**
   Contact The Disney Channel at (818) 569-7533.
   Awards of $2,500 to honor classroom projects on diversity

6. **Aspire Higher Grants for Girls**
   Contact the Women's Sports Foundation at (800) 227-3988.
   Funds projects for girls, $250–500

7. **AT&T Foundation Learning Network Grants**
   Contact the Regional Contributions Manager if you live in a
   city with a high concentration of AT&T employees.

8. **Barbara Bush Foundation for Family Literacy**
   http://www.barbarabushfoundation.com/geninfo.html
   (202) 955-6183
   Grants up to $50,000 for family literacy projects

9. **Bell Atlantic Foundation Grants**
   Apply online at www.bellatlantic.com for grants in
   education and fine arts in Maine to Virginia.

10. **Bell South Net Day Grants**
    Apply on the Bell South web site at www.bellsouth.com
    for $500 mini-grants for classroom technology.

11. **Annie E. Casey Foundation**
    (410) 223-2891
    Grants that affect public policy for children

12. **Clorox Company Foundation**
    Visit the web site at www.clorox.com for information on
    education grants given in communities where Clorox has a
    corporate presence (15 states).

13. **Coca Cola Foundation**
    Write to: P.O. Box 734, Atlanta, GA 30301
    Grants in the fields of teaching and learning or global education

14. **Compaq Computer Corporation**
    Write to: Coordinator,
    Box 692000-040511, Houston, TX 77269-2000
    Equipment donations only

15. **Constitutional Rights Foundation**
    (213) 487-5590
    Service-learning grants up to $1,000

16. **Corporation for Public Broadcasting**
    Visit the web site at: http://www.cpb.org
    Grants for stand-alone educational programs to air on
    public television

17. **Creative Classroom/Plan a Dream Grants**
    Write to: Children's Television Workshop,
    One Lincoln Plaza, New York, NY 10023
    $2,500 grants for classroom innovations

18. **The Charles A. Dana Foundation and The Dana
    Alliance for Brain Initiatives**
    Visit the web site at http://www.dana.org for larger grants for
    early childhood education.

19. **DOW/NTSA Summer Chemistry Workshop**
    (703) 243-7100
    Call to find the cost of sending teachers to the program.

20. **The Duke Endowment**
    Call (704) 376-0291, or visit the web site at
    www.dukeendowment.org for projects for child welfare in
    North and South Carolina (especially private schools).

21. **Education's Unsung Hero Awards**
    Fax: (507) 931-9709
    Cash awards and scholarships for outstanding teachers

22. **Excellence in Teaching Cabinet Grants**
    Visit the web site at:
    http://www.curriculumassociates.com/cabinet/cabinetintro.shtml
    Grants of $1,000, plus $500 gift certificates for K–8 excellence
    in teaching

23. **Exxon Foundation Education Grants**
    Visit the web site at www.exxon.com for math grants in the
    amount of $10,000 or more to improve mathematics education.

24. First Union Seeds for Success Education Grants
http://www.firstunion.com/involve/involvement/education/
education.html
Grants of $1,000 to $10,000
Requires partnership with First Union employees

25. Foundation for Exceptional Children
(703) 620-1054
Grants of $500

26. The GE Fund
Write for annual report and guidelines to:
GE Fund, 3135 Easton Turnpike, Fairfield, CT 06431
Funds programs in child welfare and science education

27. Georgia Schoolyard Wildlife Habitat Grants
Contact the Wildlife Resources Division at (770) 784-3059.
Grants of $2,500 for outdoor classrooms

28. Hartford Foundation for Public Giving
(860) 548-1888
School grants in the Hartford, CT area

29. Hasbro Children's Foundation
(212) 645-2400
Direct focus on children, birth to 12 years

30. The Kellogg Foundation
(616) 968-1611
Education grants

31. Lifetouch Enrichment Grants
Write for an application to:
141 South 7th St., Minneapolis, MN 55402
$2,500 mini-grants for teachers

32. John D. and Catherine T. MacArthur Foundation
Fax: (312) 920-6258
Grants for education of $10,000 or larger

33. Microsoft in K–12 Education Grants
Visit the web site at:
http://www.microsoft.com/education/schools
Technology grants and free training for teachers

34. National Arts Education Foundation

Write to: NAEF, 1916 Association Dr., Reston, VA 22091-1590
Several art education grant programs available to association members only.

35. National Gardening Association Grants

(802) 863-1308
Grants of $500

36. National Geographic Society

Visit the web site at: http://www.nationalgeographic.com
Awards of $12,500

37. National Science Foundation

(703) 306-1234
Many programs available.
Also see NSF web site at:
http://www.nsf.gov/home/grants.htm

38. National Science Teaching Award

Write to: NSTA, 1840 Wilson Blvd., Arlington, VA 22201-3000
Shell Oil Company awards of $10,000

39. JC Penney Community Education Grants

(972) 431-1349
Curriculum development grants of $5,000 to $50,000

40. JC Penney Golden Rule Award

(972) 431-1319
Grants of $1,000 to local educators

41. Scholastic "Mrs. Frizzle" Grants

Write to: Scholastic Inc., 555 Broadway, New York, NY 10012
Awards of $5,000 cash and $5,000 in books

42. Second Chance Equipment Grants

Contact the Women's Sports Foundation at (800) 227-3988.
Used sports equipment grants

43. Southern Early Childhood Association

(800) 305-7322
Grants $1,000 awards for curriculum and staff development to members and affiliates

44. State Farm Insurance Good Neighbor Awards
Contact the National Council for the Social Studies at (202) 966-7840.
Grants $5,000 awards to social studies teachers of excellence

45. Technology Literacy Challenge Grants
Visit the United States Department of Education home page at http://www.ed.gov/Technology/ to find out about block grants to your state to improve technology in the schools.

46. Thinkquest Grants
Visit the Thinkquest web site at: www.thinkquest.org/
Grants $1 million in awards and scholarships for teams of middle school students to design web pages.

47. Toshiba America Foundation
Visit the Toshiba web site www.toshiba.com for science and math education improvements.

48. Toyota Tapestry Grants
(800) 807-9852
Science grants of $10,000

49. Toyota TIME Grants
(888) 573-8463
Math initiatives for schools

50. UPS Foundation
(404) 828-6451
Funds literacy projects

51. Wal-Mart Foundation
Write to: Coordinator, 702 S.W. Eighth St., Bentonville, AR 72716-8071

Note: At the time of the preparation of this book, the web sites, telephone numbers, and addresses were current and the grants were available. Please keep in mind the fact that information and grant resources, especially web sites, are subject to change.

I made an effort to show you a variety of grants for subject area, size of grants, and funding sources. Read on to find out more about using these sources wisely and efficiently.

Important Notes About the 51 Sources

- Call or write for project guidelines and applications.

- Do not send a grant proposal directly to any of the sources listed.

- Some grants, especially mini-grants, now require an online or electronic submission.

- Some large corporations only award grants in an area where they have a corporate presence.

- Many large foundations give larger grants ($10,000 or more), but these grants will probably require a research component and a university partner.

- A local grant, such as the Georgia Wildlife grant for outdoor classrooms, probably is similar to a grant program in your region. Call your local wildlife groups.

- Many associations that offer grants limit their awards to members and affiliates. It pays to keep your professional organizations and affiliations current.

- Grants can take on different names—*awards, incentives, initiatives, scholarships, gifts.*

- Many banks and financial institutions have grant programs. Call your local financial institutions to inquire about mini-grants.

- There is a trend in larger cities to consolidate giving programs into a local community foundation such as that listed for Hartford, CT. In Charleston, SC, it is the Lowcountry Community Foundation. Look in your phone book's white pages for a similar organization or call the chamber of commerce.

- Some grants are for "equipment only."

- Many of the larger grants will require matching funds and a history of prior grants.

- When you call, or write, or visit the web site for the grant application or guidelines, look for key terms such as *limitations, mission statement,* and *goals* to find out if the source is a match for you.

The Quest for Public Money

Federal and state money is what I call "public money." Our tax dollars fill the coffers out of which these grants are awarded.

Federal grants are usually larger grants ($10,000 or more) and require technical, cumbersome proposal writing. Typically, large federal grants are not written by teachers. They are written by school district grant writers or professional consultants who may work with a team of teachers. The best thing for a teacher or novice grant writer to do if he or she wants to learn about federal grants for schools is to request a free copy of a nifty little blue book that I found on the Internet called *What Should I Know About ED Grants?* It is a government publication and you can get it through the U.S. Department of Education web site at www.ed.gov/, or by simply writing a postcard to the United States Department of Education, Washington, DC 20503.

You can also call 1-800-688-9889 and ask for a copy of this book and other grant-related information from additional federal agencies, such as the Department of Energy or the Department of Health and Human Services. This number connects grant writers to the Federal Information Center. There is also a nifty new web site: http://fic.info.gov/. I recommend this source, because your school might qualify for grants "through the back door," that is, from an agency not directly related to education but that targets children and youth. For example, I got grant dollars to fund a wonderful summer math program for gifted middle school girls by using money from the DOE (Department of Energy), which was trying to recruit future engineers by interesting girls in math and science.

Once you have read this free blue book, you will be better equipped to actually look at what is available from the government. Make sure that you thoroughly review the glossary of grant terms (pages A-1 to A-9). It is best to learn the language before you move into the federal web site.

The web site that you need is called the Federal Register. This site shows you what the U.S. Department of Education is currently offering. The address is: http://www.access.gpo.gov/su_docs/.

I like to check out this site regularly just to see what's cooking. Recently, there was a run on special education grants to service "transition students" (see "The Top 10 Hot Topics for Grants," page 23).

Once you are in the Federal Register online, make sure to "bookmark" the site, or add it to your favorites, then start browsing. It is a good idea to look for your specific department, such as elementary education or bilingual education. Grants tend to be quite specific.

A word of caution, however. These large federal grants are provided to accomplish a particular task, address needs, or to serve a preselected group of citizens. You cannot get "big federal grants" just to make your school's dreams come true. You have to match your need to what the government currently considers as a priority. In looking for federal money, as in most grant writing, you will find that most of your work comes in the form of research, not writing. It is essential to make a good match.

In addition, you will notice that federal grants move in cycles. It is common to have to qualify for a "seed money" grant or an experimental cycle of funding first, rather than what is called "full implementation." The government wants to see how you do with a little money for a year, to try your idea with a control group or in one school before they pour a considerable number of dollars into a leaky pot! Also, don't be surprised if you have to try for several cycles before you are awarded a grant. It is tough to get funded the first time around.

Moreover, federal money moves down into the states in the form of "block grants" and competitive grants. Use your state's web site to find out about these funds. Eisenhower math and science money is an example of this funding. In many states, there is a grant coordinator who works with schools and agencies. It is a good idea to invite this coordinator to your school to do a staff development workshop and make contact with your group.

Public money is not "all dried up" as some claim. It is still around, but it is more specific to needs of individual groups or to educational priorities, such as technology or special education. It won't fund everything you need, but it might be the right match for a particular goal in your district's strategic plan.

Federal grants are usually "big grants," in terms of funding and preparation. Read the next section to find out if you are ready to go after a "big grant."

Following the Hierarchy of Grants

Grants come in many shapes and sizes. There is a general rule of thumb, however. You need to practice on mini-grants of $25 to $1,000; polish your skills on small to medium grants $1,000 to $10,000; and then try for a "big grant" ($10,000 and up). These numbers represent my personal experience with grants. This is how I see them breaking down.

There are some specific reasons why one should follow the hierarchy of grant getting:

Skill. Grant writing is a skill that takes time and practice to develop. You don't want to make a bad impression on a potentially generous funding source by sending a weak proposal.

History. All of the big corporate or federal grant applications that I have seen require a history or discussion of the grants you have already been awarded for your school and/or for similar projects.

Experience. Without adequate experience and/or the assistance of a grant consultant, you probably won't have the knowledge of grants that it will take to complete the details for a large proposal.

Experimentation. Many "big grants" are awarded after the successful completion of a "seed money" or practice grant in which you try out the idea or initiative in one school before you bring in the entire district.

Research. "Big grants" almost always require some research. This means: (1) a robust body of research that supports the need for your projects, and (2) a research component that your grant will accomplish. Most groups or schools need to build up the connections with universities or hospitals that it takes to pull off this kind of grant.

Teamwork. "Big grants" almost always require *collaboration*. This is a hot trend in grant writing. The grant is awarded to two or more groups, or agencies, to accomplish the goals, affect many children, and gain a wider recognition for the funder. Again, it takes time and other grant experience to build these relationships.

Change. "Big grants" are about *systemic change.* Again, this is a hot term in grant writing. If you want a large amount of money, you have to convince the funder that you will change the entire system, or the way things are done, in your school, program, or area of expertise. Again, it takes a history of smaller grants to build up the evidence you need to justify the claim to systemic change.

So, do you really need, want, or have the "right stuff" to go after a "big grant"? Maybe not today, but if you use the resources in this book appropriately, you will!

Remember, it takes "many drops to make a flood." Be patient and persistent, and take a look at the marvelous sample grants in Chapter Five to find out how teachers just like you are building their credentials as grant writers.

Date _____

Do You Have the "Right Stuff"?

Directions: Stop and take some notes. Are you ready for a "big grant"? Complete these prompts.

My experience with grants has been . . .

_____

_____

Our school's funding history is . . .

_____

_____

We are prepared to do or support research by . . .

_____

_____

Our plan includes *systemic change* in the form of . . .

_____

_____

We have a plan for *collaboration* in the form of . . .

_____

_____

Chapter Five: Samples of Winning Grant Proposals

Words of Wisdom

66*Seeing once is*

better than

*hearing twice.*99

—*Swedish Saying*

In the last chapter of *The Grant Writer's Guide,* you have the unique opportunity to look at some real grants written by extraordinary teachers.

There are seven sample grants representing a variety of grade levels and targeting different student groups.

Keep in mind that these grants must not be copied. That would be unethical. Instead, you are invited to take a look at how these seven teachers used language, organized their proposals, and tapped into research to design a winning grant.

Each sample grant is unique. For the sake of space, I did not give you the complete grant, including budgets and addenda for every grant. Instead, I showed samples so you can get an idea of what is fundable.

Before you review the proposals, consider these notes:

- Notice how the teachers emphasized the catchy title throughout the narrative.

- Notice their use of headings to organize the proposal.

- Notice the match between objectives and evaluation criteria.

- Notice the specific activities and how they are related to the budgets.

- Notice the use of research and letters of support to justify the need for the projects.

- Notice the marketing strategies in the dissemination plans.

These grants are not edited to be "picture perfect." They were written by teachers in public schools and were funded in highly competitive situations. Several of the grants have been rewritten by the teacher, resubmitted, and funded in a number of different grant competitions. The names of the teachers are listed in the table of contents, and their contributions make this book valuable and credible.

Introduce Your Proposal

The letter of intent is used to introduce your project to the potential funder. It usually accompanies an abstract. There are several project abstracts in the sample grants.

Address of Funding Source

Dear _____ (Grants Officer):

We are pleased to submit this abstract of Project (Title), which represents a partnership between the Anywhere County School District, the Big University, and the Regional Technology Consortium.

This group of educational partners is seeking funding in the amount of $100,000 to integrate the use of technology, including the Internet, in 10 middle and high schools in our district.

The attached abstract offers an overview of the project and its expected outcomes. We look forward to submitting a full proposal during the next funding cycle if this abstract meets your approval.

Please direct your questions and feedback to Ms. Linda Bone, Project Coordinator. She can be reached by e-mail at lbone@csuniv.edu, or by telephone at (XXX)XXX-XXXX. We look forward to a positive response.

Yours truly,

Linda K. Bone
Project Coordinator

Project Title: Private "I" on Science

Funds Requested: $1,932.00

Project Abstract

Young children are natural investigators. They use all of their senses to investigate, inquire, and interpret the world around them. This innovative EIA proposal, **Private "I" on Science**, places 22 first-grade students at Anyville Elementary School in the role of "private investigator," using the science process skills of inquiry to investigate and interpret the natural world. Hence, these youngsters use their "eyes" to complete the "I-tasks" that make science so meaningful. The funds will be used to purchase life cycle puppets, science big book sets, a saltwater aquarium, Seed to Plant science module centers, a 3-D microscope, critter jars, and other investigative support items. These materials will be used to complete three units of first-grade life science study as outlined in the Anywhere County Science Curriculum. These three units include: Animal Wonders Under the Sea, Land Animal Habitats and Life Cycles, and Plant Life from Seed to Maturity. Using standardized assessment instruments such as checklists, tasks, and rubrics, students' comprehension will be regularly evaluated in the areas of scientific knowledge and application.

Overview of the Project and Needs Statement

Why should we want to put our children in basic science studies at such an early age? To understand the scope of the problems we are facing, one must understand the culture at Anyville Elementary School. It is a large suburban school of approximately 800 students located in Anywhere County. Thirty-two percent of our students receive free or reduced-rate lunch as they come from impoverished, or lower income, families. Our children are loved by their parents; however, most of them come from two-income families. Because of their hurried family lives, they have not had a rich set of early childhood experiences. Their exposure to the wonders of the ocean, the life cycles of animals, and the growing and nurturing of plants has been severely limited. It is our belief that **Private "I" on Science** modules will greatly enrich the lives of these young students and will help them recognize the fascinating nature of the physical and life sciences.

Qualitative and quantitative data have been collected to support the need for this project. Specifically, science scores in the area of life science demonstrate serious comprehension problems. Last year, our third-grade students dropped over 30 percentage points in the sciences. Our state is ranked in the bottom 10 percent of the nation for science scores on standardized tests. Also, qualitative data has been collected from a life science pretest (Addendum I)* administered to first-grade students. The results indicate a critical need for students to be exposed to the life sciences. It has been documented in numerous scientific journals and in our curriculum guides that hands-on investigations are the most successful exercises to communicate science concepts to young children.

Finally, the importance of Project **Private "I" on Science** can be underscored by a letter of support from Ms. Kathy S____, a Science Specialist at the _____ Math and Science Hub (see Addendum II)*. She states, "There is simply no substitute for high quality investigative science experiences for young children. The opportunity for students to begin their educational careers with science opportunities such as this will serve as the genesis for a rich and full science program."

Goals and Objectives

Goal: The goal of **Private "I" on Science** is to introduce first-grade students to the science process skills through hands-on investigative experiences with live plants and animals.

Objectives: The funding of **Private "I" on Science** will result in the following:

Objective One: Students will complete a unit of study on land animal life cycles and their habitats.

Objective Two: Students will complete a unit of study on ocean animals and their environments.

Objective Three: Students will complete a unit of study on plant life from seed to maturity.

Relationship of Objectives to Curriculum Frameworks

Project **Private "I" on Science** will apply and strengthen the goals established within "The Vision for Science Education" as noted in the South Carolina Frameworks. This project will prepare students to meet the National Education Goal #5, which states, "By the year 2000, United States students will be the first in the world in mathematics and science achievement."

The Anywhere County School District Strategic Plan Strategy #1 states, "We will design and implement a student-centered curriculum that focuses on creativity, communication, and lifelong learning. Action Plan #70 states, "The future will ensure that all students, grades kindergarten through eighth, will fully participate in the hands-on, experimental, board-adopted science curriculum. Project **Private "I" on Science** will encompass and enhance these strategic plans to better the science education curriculum in the Anywhere County School District.

Sample Activities

Project **Private "I" on Science** will include numerous hands-on and investigative activities. Listed on the following page is a description of activities from each unit.

Activity One: Students will read a variety of **science literature** in a science center designated by the **area rug that depicts the ladybug's life cycle.**

Activity Two: Groups of students will build a **saltwater aquarium** to observe the communities of **saltwater plants and animals** undergo life-cycle and food-chain interactions.

Activity Three: Students will describe and classify **seeds** by properties, while observing and recording plant growth. Students will investigate the functions of plant parts and plant responses to environmental factors.

Activity Four: Students will make observations of **plant parts and insects** using the **3-D microscope.**

Activity Five: Students will observe the life cycle of the butterfly from inside the **Butterfly Pavilion.** After the **painted lady butterflies** emerge from their chrysalises, the Butterfly Pavilion tent will be taken outside for the release of the butterflies.

Activity Six: Students will dive into the world of ocean animals through the use of the computer program **Undersea Adventure.** Realistic sounds, color images, and an encyclopedia about the ocean with interactive links will be used daily with the Wonders Under the Sea unit.

Time Line for the Project

July 1996	Order materials.
August 1996	Organize the materials in the science lab and prepare a teacher's guide for each of the life science units.
September 1996	Conduct a first-grade teachers in-service to introduce Project **Private "I" on Science** and train teachers how to use the life science materials. Administer the life science pretest (Addendum I)* to first-grade students.
October 1996	Conduct science experiences in animal habitats and life cycles.
November 1996	First-grade classes will visit Riverbanks Zoo in Columbia, South Carolina.
December 1996	Administer the Land Animal Habitat and Life Cycle post-test.
January 1997	Conduct hands-on science experiences of ocean animals and their environments.
February 1997	First-grade classes visit Marine Resource Center on James Island, South Carolina. Administer the Animal Wonders Under the Sea post-test.
March 1997	Conduct hands-on activities and science experiences with plants from seeds to maturity.
April 1997	First-grade classes visit Middleton Place Plantation and Gardens in Charleston, South Carolina. Administer the Plant Life from Seeds to Maturity post-test.
May 1997	Prepare the final report of the success of the **Private "I" on Science** project.

Evaluation Plan

The evaluation plan for Project **Private "I" on Science** includes the following outcomes:

Evaluation One: By the end of the project year 1997, all of the participating students will achieve 90 percent accuracy on the Land Animal Habitats and Life Cycles post-test.

Evaluation Two: By the end of the project year 1997, all the participating students will achieve 90 percent accuracy on the Wonders Under the Sea post-test.

Evaluation Three: By the end of the project year 1997, all participating students will achieve 90 percent accuracy on the Plant Life from Seed to Maturity post-test.

The development of science knowledge and application is not always measurable in terms of percentages. In addition to the previous evaluations, a Science Checklist (Addendum III)*, Science Chats: A Response Log (Addendum IV)*, and science rubrics will be used on a regular basis throughout Project **Private "I" on Science** as additional ways to assess students' progress.

Exportable Product/Dissemination Plan

The exportable product of Project **Private "I" on Science** will be a wide assortment of life science materials conveniently set up in the Anyville Elementary School Science Lab. Teachers will be supplied with a life science teacher's guide for each of the three units of study. Step-by-step instructions for hands-on activities, investigations, and experiences using the science process skills will be included. Each teacher will receive pretest and post-test assessments, along with the attached Addenda I*, III*, and IV*.

Follow-up and/or Dissemination of Results

Dissemination of information derived from Project **Private "I" on Science** is included in my personal plan for professional development. ADEPT, our new guideline for teacher evaluation, includes PD 10: Professional Development. To fulfill this requirement, I will train and share Project **Private "I" on Science** with the six other first-grade teachers at Anyville Elementary School. I also plan to present this project at the Fall 1997 Anywhere County School District Teacher In-Service, using photographs and videos of students applying their scientific knowledge and hands-on skills during various activities funded by this grant. The teaching guide for each **Private "I" on Science** unit will be made available to all interested teachers in the district at that time.

Supporting Information: Addenda

These are descriptions of the actual addenda included with this proposal.

Addendum I*
Example of Life Science Pretest to establish students' prior knowledge

Addendum II*
Letter of Support for the **Private "I" on Science** Grant from Math and Science Hub Science Specialist

Addendum III*
Example of Science Checklist to monitor students' behavior and record teacher's observations

Addendum IV*
Example of Science Chats: A Response Log to record students' observations

*Addenda are not included for this example.

Project Title: Let's Go GEO!

Amount Requested: $1,931.32

Needs Statement

Anyville Elementary School is a fairly large (817 students), rural, ethnically diverse school, with 57.1 percent of the students receiving free or reduced-rate lunch. In the fall of 1997, we will be moving to a new school. The budget constraints that this will create will greatly limit the funds available for any additional materials or programs to be implemented in the classroom. However, as indicated, there is a strong need for an intense language-enriched geography program as presented in this proposal, **Let's Go GEO!**

Based on the Geography Skills pretest, administered during the spring of 1997, 64 percent of the students could not identify the four major oceans of the world, 63 percent could not locate the continent on which they live, and 85 percent could not label a major river in the United States. (Addendum I)* Moreover, our students demonstrate significant need in language and language development as illustrated in the following chart.

Expressive Language	**Total Language**	**Remedial Services**
54% below national average in expressive language battery	52% below national average in total language battery	87 students being remediated

The attached article suggests that American school children seem "lost in their native land" and reports that "geography has been losing ground, particularly in our primary and secondary schools." The article further states that "geography must find its way back into the schools of America, and once there, it must be promoted and maintained." (Addendum II)*

A letter from Linda G___, professor of history and geography at Charleston Southern University, documents the need for innovation such as **Let's Go GEO!** in meeting the learning needs of second-grade students. (Addendum III)* This proposal brings a language-rich geography curriculum to Anyville Elementary School. It is anticipated that the magnetic kits, maps, atlases, hands-on activities and manipulatives, and other innovative practices will boost test scores and the pure knowledge of geography of 240 second-grade students, making **Let's Go GEO!** an inexpensive, yet powerful curriculum tool.

Goal

To provide an integrated language–geography program in 10 second-grade classes. This program will increase students' knowledge base of pure geography through a language-experience approach.

Objectives

1. Each student will demonstrate improvement in vocabulary and language usage as measured by the SAT-8/MAT-7.

2. Each student will demonstrate an increase in his or her knowledge of pure geography. (Addendum I)*

3. By the end of the project year 1998, each student will produce a **Let's Go GEO!** portfolio containing samples of work related to language expression and geography knowledge. (Addendum V)*

4. Students will exhibit an understanding of various geographic locations and the characteristics of each. (Addendum V)*

5. Each student will apply geography to relate his or her present to their origins.

Relationship of Objectives to Curriculum Frameworks or School/District Renewal Plan

There is no adopted South Carolina Framework for social studies; however, according to the National Geography Standards adopted in 1994, "knowledge of geography enables people to develop an understanding of the relationships between people,

© Good Apple GA13054

places, and environments over time—that is, of Earth as it was, is, and might be." It states that the geographically-informed person should know how to apply geography to interpret the past and present, and plan for the future. It goes on to say that "people are central to geography in that human activities help shape Earth's surface, human settlements and structures are part of Earth's surface, and humans compete for control of Earth's surface."

As stated in the Strategic Planning School Improvement Report for Anyville Elementary School, it is our goal to "insure that every child develops to his or her maximum potential" and to "create an academic setting that is non-threatening, nurturing, helps foster an attitude of pride in the school and a love for learning." The Strategic Plan, focusing on history and geography, adds that "the social studies program is integrated throughout the curriculum," and that "Daily Oral Geography is used as an instructional tool and strategy that helps students answer questions about world geography." Implementation of this proposal, **Let's Go GEO!**, will be a vital addition to the ongoing instruction of geography in the second-grade classes at our school.

Finally, research completed by the South Carolina State Development Board confirms that several countries have investments in South Carolina. These countries include Australia, Austria, Belgium, Brazil, Canada, Denmark, Egypt, Finland, France, Germany, India, Ireland, Italy, Japan, Korea, Kuwait, Luxembourg, Mexico, the Netherlands, Northern Ireland, Spain, Sweden, Switzerland, Taiwan, the United Kingdom, and Venezuela. As stated in the South Carolina Foreign Languages Frameworks, developed by the Curriculum Framework Writing Team and adopted by the South Carolina State Board of Education in November 1993, "It is the responsibility of the state's education system to prepare students to compete in an increasingly international job market and to live in an increasingly diverse world." But how are our students to compete in this market if they do not even know where these countries are? To be successful in the 21st century, we need to expand not only the basic skills of our students, but also the boundaries of their environments. It is important that this expansion and an interest in geography begin early in a student's education. **Let's Go GEO!** has been designed to do just that.

Program Strategy/Activities

Note: All bold-face items are purchased with grant funds.

I. Big Book Atlases
Using **atlas activity and enrichment programs**, along with **continent theme units**, students will work cooperatively to create big book atlases to be added to classroom libraries.

II. Vacation Time
Students will use *Magnetic Way* **boards and maps** to share their favorite vacations.

III. Parent Days
Parents will be invited for Awards Day at the end of each nine week grading period. Students will share *Let's Go GEO!* activities and **portfolio** entries at this time.

IV. GEO-Dictionaries
Using **three-ring binders**, students will maintain class geography dictionaries, entering information that is found while using *Let's Go GEO!* activities and **discovery atlases**. These dictionaries will be kept in a **book display stand** for easy access.

V. The Sands of Time
Students will work in small groups, locating and researching deserts, and then give oral presentations using the **Exploring Deserts** *Magnetic Way* **overlay kit**.

VI. Water, Water Everywhere!
Students will locate and research the oceans of the world and do oral presentations using the **Exploring Oceans** *Magnetic Way* **overlay kit**.

VII. Jungle Journey
Students will locate and research the world's rain forests and give oral presentations using the **Exploring Rain Forests** *Magnetic Way* **overlay kit**.

VIII. Conferencing
A time will be set aside before each presentation for the students and teacher to discuss the presentations to be given.

IX. Where Would I Go?
U.S. and World jumbo puzzles will be used to locate students' "Dream Journeys." Students will place puzzle pieces in the correct locations and then tell about their destinations and all the exciting things that will happen there.

X. Student Journals
Students will keep personal journals, using **pocket portfolios**, to record their geography "discoveries." These will be used as positive feedback for peers.

XI. Host Class
Using the **overlay kits for deserts, oceans, and rain forests**, students will work in small groups to write stories and practice presentations of these stories. Kindergarten and first-grade classes will be invited to enjoy these presentations.

XII. I'm From . . .
Students will use **maps and globes** to present to their classmates a brief oral report about their family tree exhibits.

Note: The activities for *Let's Go GEO!* meet the guidelines set forth in the *National Geography Standards,* especially 1, 4, and 17. Also incorporated are language arts, language development, and social studies skills established in the *Strategic Plan for Anyville Elementary School,* along with objectives outlined in the Anywhere County curriculum for language arts, including reading, writing, reference skills, and public speaking. Each activity is aligned to the evaluations as outlined in the Evaluations section.

Time Line for the Project

August 1997	Order materials.
August 1997	Set up **Let's Go GEO!** area in classroom.
August 1997	In-service for second-grade teachers to implement grant.
August 1997	Administer and record results of pretest.
September 1997	Send informational letter to parents describing the project.
September 1997	Create schedule for oceans, deserts, and rain forest presentations.
October 1997	Parent Day/first nine weeks
November 1997	"The Sands of Time" small-group presentations
December 1997	Follow-up in-service for second-grade teachers.
January 1998	Create schedule for second semester paired presentations.
January 1998	Parent Day/second nine weeks
February 1998	"Water, Water Everywhere!" small-group presentations
March 1998	Parent Day/third nine weeks
March 1998	Begin "Family Tree" exhibit displays.
April 1998	"Jungle Journey" small-group presentations
April 1998	Schedule and begin Host Class stories and presentations to kindergarten and first-grade classes.
May 1998	Administer and record results of post-test.
May 1998	Parent Day/fourth nine weeks
May 1998	Portfolio Party
May 1998	Collect sample portfolios to submit for final report.

Evaluations

1. By the end of the project year 1998, each student will demonstrate a five-point increase on the test of vocabulary/language development.

2. Using a pre-post application of the geography instrument, each student will demonstrate at least 80 percent mastery of the information. (Addendum I)*

3. Using language development and social studies rubrics, products from **Let's Go GEO!** will be evaluated to show growth in language and geography knowledge. (Addendum IV)*

4. Using the *Magnetic Way* program and working in small groups, each group will research and make presentations with the following themes: Exploring Deserts, Exploring Oceans, Exploring Rain Forests, and Regional Geography of the United States.

5. Each student will investigate his or her family tree. Using maps and globes, each student will create a family history exhibit, including geographical location, climate, physical environment, natural resources, and products/industry of the country of his or her origin.

Dissemination of Information

A portfolio will be kept for each student and will contain products from material gathered using **Let's Go GEO!**, samples of students' work, pre- and post-test results, evaluation instruments (quiz and test results), as well as attitude sheets to record students' feelings about selected assignments. Using social studies and language arts checklists and a rubric to measure individual performance, students' geography and language progress will be evaluated throughout the year, with a final evaluation at the end of the year. This will give students an opportunity to share their work with their families, administrators, and other teachers and students.

Exportable Product

1. Two in-service training sessions for 10 second-grade teachers to implement **Let's Go GEO!** in each classroom, including a list of materials available and instructions on how to use them.

2. A video, *Where in the World is Anyville Elementary School?*, a take off on the popular *Carmen San Diego* theme. The video will introduce **Let's Go GEO!** method and include a segment that will show students demonstrating the program and materials.

3. A copy of the above mentioned video will be placed in the Language Arts Department of Anyville County Schools.

4. Each child will take home a bound atlas at the end of the project year 1998.

*Addenda are not included for this example.

Budget Breakdown

Magnetic Way Overlay Kits

Exploring Deserts	$129.00
Exploring Oceans	129.00
Exploring Rain Forests	129.00
Regional Geography	165.00
Looking at Our Communities	129.00
U.S. Jumbo Floor Puzzle	34.99
World Jumbo Floor Puzzle	29.99
Map and Globe Skills for Basic Beginners	66.00
World Discovery Atlases —5 @$9.95	49.75
U.S. Discovery Atlases—5 @$9.95	49.75
Beginning Geography Reproducible Activities	5.95
Big Book of Maps	19.95
Continents Theme Unit	34.99
U.S. Theme Unit	34.99
Giant Atlas Package	60.00
Basic Classroom Set U.S./World Maps/15" Globe	313.00
Classroom Atlas Enrichment Program	239.00
Twin Pocket Portfolios—2 pkgs. @$6.95	13.90
Construction Paper, 12" x 18"—10 pkgs. @$1.94	9.40
Vinyl Ring Binders with 1-inch rings—4 @$5.50	8.20
Video Cassette Tapes—4 @$5.50	22.00
Book Display Stand	119.00
Allowance for Shipping and Handling	140.00
TOTAL	$1,931.86

Sample Grant Proposal
Abstract

Project Title: Historical Heroines for Today's Girls

Amount Requested: $6,000.00

Today's girls often grow up too fast, especially in the isolated, rural area of Anywhere County where we teach. We have problems with teen pregnancy, high school dropouts, and violence against women. Our project takes a simple, yet sound approach toward changing these paradigms. **Historical Heroines for Today's Girls** uses a series of popular, appealing children's stories about girls who are strong and independent, along with props, lessons, role-playing, and celebrations to build self-esteem, self-awareness, and academic skills among fifth-grade girls at Anyville Elementary School.

We are requesting funds in the amount of $6,000 to establish the project that will impact approximately 100 girls in a motivational enrichment program. The girls will be encouraged to join the "Historical Heroines Reading Club," which will meet every two weeks during the teachers' planning periods. The girls will read the novels included in Historical Handbags—canvas bags containing one of the books, the matching "American Girl doll," accessories, and learning activities. The groups will also have guest speakers, women from the community who will speak on local history and folklore.

With some of the lowest academic test scores in the region, a 99 percent rate for free and reduced-rate lunches, and other critical data, which will be illuminated in the full proposal, we have an excellent rationale for funding.

Historical Heroines for Today's Girls will emerge as a model program for rural schools that serve high numbers of disadvantaged students, and will result in greater literacy and confidence among the students. We look forward to the opportunity to submit a full proposal.

Project Title: Wise Buys

Funds Requested: $1,907.00

Project Summary

Wise Buys is an innovative state teacher grant proposal to implement a consumer mathematics curriculum within the sixth-grade classes at Anyville Elementary School. The students will gain confidence in performing everyday tasks that require math by utilizing daily hands-on experiences gained in the classroom. They will design and run a class store, take field trips to banks and grocery stores, create menus and purchase items to prepare dinners for needy families, maintain and balance a checkbook, and complete a text entitled *Math for Everyday Living*. They will investigate practical mathematical concepts such as addition, subtraction, fractions, decimals, and so on. They will investigate basic banking concepts such as budgeting for expenditures, computing interest, applying for credit, balancing a checkbook, and so on. They will have the opportunity to practice and reinforce hands-on experiences with the use of the textbooks and classroom centers. At the bank, students will learn about banking services such as checking accounts, certificates of deposit, and the automated teller. At the grocery store, students will do price comparisons in order to buy items for food baskets for four needy families at Thanksgiving time. Each group will have a budget of $100.00 to spend on its food basket. Students will use a checkbook and register to keep up with spending. Students will organize and run a school store. They will be responsible for purchasing items to be sold in the store, selling the goods, and keeping track of the inventory. The **Wise Buys** program will make wise consumers out of sixth graders who typically have no concept of how quickly money can be spent or how important it is to learn how to manage money wisely.

Justification for the Project

The setting for **Wise Buys** is Anyville Elementary School. Anyville Elementary School is a small community school located in a rural, remote area of Anywhere County. The majority of students within the school come from minority groups, with a mix of 75 percent black and 25 percent white. Ninety-six percent of the students at this school receive free or reduced-rate lunch.

There is little money, opportunity, or interest among families in enriching the experiences of their young children. Children seldom have the opportunity to learn how to manage money. Parents have just enough money to get by. There are few "extras" to enable 11-year-olds to receive an allowance or set up a bank account. Some parents do not feel comfortable talking about money with their children. They consider it something for "adults to worry about." Therefore, children grow up thinking money is a problem or something to worry about. They don't see it as a commodity they can learn to control.

Test scores in mathematics reveal the need for **Wise Buys**, with 56 percent of fifth graders at Anyville Elementary not meeting the national average for computation and problem-solving on the MAT-7. (Addendum I)*

Finally, **Wise Buys** is recognized by Mrs. Mary J___, president of the local bank, as an important curriculum addition that will help youngsters gain confidence and skill in managing their future finances. Her letter of support is attached.*

Goal, Objectives, and Evaluation Measures

The goal of the **Wise Buys** program is to enable students to see the relevance to their own lives of consumer math skills taught within the classroom. They will also become wise consumers.

Objective 1: Students will design and operate a class store.

Evaluation: Students will work in the class store ordering and pricing supplies, selling to customers, and keeping track of inventory.

Objective 2: Students will maintain and balance a checkbook.

Evaluation: Students will turn in their checkbooks at the end of the program, and the teacher will check them for accuracy.

Objective 3: Students will create a menu for a Thanksgiving dinner by using computation and planning skills.

Evaluation: From the menu, students will make a list of items needed for the dinner and purchase these items at the appropriate grocery store. The teacher will assess their lists for accuracy.

Objective 4: Students will improve their math computation and application skills.

Evaluation: By the end of the project year, participating students will complete all 10 chapters of the math skills practice book to 90 percent accuracy. This skills practice book contains exercises involving math computation and skills practice. Also, by the end of the project year, we anticipate an increase of three to five percentage points on the MAT-7 math achievement test.

Objective 5: Students will take a field trip to the bank to learn about banking services.

Evaluation: Students will make a list of banking jobs. They will prepare a list of math skills they observed being used at the bank on the day of the field trip.

Relationship of Objectives to State Curriculum Guidelines

The objectives for **Wise Buys** show a relationship to the NCTM (National Council of Teachers of Mathematics) Curriculum and Evaluation Standards for School Mathematics and the South Carolina Mathematics Framework.

The NCTM Curriculum and Evaluation Standards for School Mathematics state:

All students must encounter mathematics through the following four processes:

- Problem Solving: solving problems in a realistic and meaningful context
- Communication: communicating with each other about what they are doing

- Reasoning: using reasoning to explain and justify their work
- Connections: make connections in their study to other aspects of mathematics and to other disciplines

For example, Objectives 1–5 meet the above conditions, following the South Carolina Mathematics Framework.

Objective 1: Operate a class store (South Carolina Framework Strand: Number and Numeration System, page 48)*

Objective 2: Maintain a checkbook (South Carolina Framework Strand: Numerical and Algebraic Concepts and Operation, page 66)*

Objective 3: Plan a Thanksgiving dinner (South Carolina Framework Strand: Pattern, Relationship, and Functions, page 68)*

Objective 4: Visit a grocery store (South Carolina Framework Strand: Pattern, Relationship, and Functions, page 68)*

Objective 5: Visit a bank (South Carolina Framework Strand: Pattern, Relationship, and Functions, page 68)*

Project Activities

The following activities will be implemented in the **Wise Buys** program.

Objective 1: Operate a class store. Students will order supplies for the store, set up a price list, plan hours of operation and a work schedule. They will maintain the inventory and will be responsible for the smooth operation of the store.

Objective 2: Maintain and balance a checkbook. Students will be taught how to set up a checking account and how to balance a checkbook.

Objective 3: Plan a Thanksgiving dinner. Students will plan a dinner and make a grocery list for the needed items.

Objective 4: Implement comparison shopping. In this activity, students will estimate the cost of several items, including taxes, and determine the amount of change from a given amount of money. Students will use newspaper advertisements to locate sale items. They will purchase identical items for the dinner and compare the prices of each item and total cost.

Objective 5: Visit a bank. Students will be divided into four groups to visit four banks within the area. As a follow-up, students will make a list of jobs available in a bank. They will explain the math skills being used at the bank. Students will discuss and compare the information obtained at each bank.

Time Line for the Project

August	Order books and supplies.
September	Set up school store. Begin unit on setting up checkbook.
October	Begin unit on earning money.
November	Plan Thanksgiving dinner. Make trip to the grocery store. Begin unit on shopping.
December	Continue unit on shopping.
January	Complete unit on buying wisely. Present workshop at district math conference.
February	Complete unit on planning a trip.
March	Complete unit on computing taxes. Complete MAT-7 testing for evaluation.
April	Complete unit on using the bank. Complete unit on trip to the bank.
May	Complete unit on buying insurance.
June	Present awards to **Wise Buys** participants.

Dissemination of the Grant

The exportable products for **Wise Buys** will be:

1. **Scrapbook:** Photos of class store, photos and narratives of the field trip

2. **Newspaper Article:** Each quarter, the teacher will write an article about the unit and field trip and send it to the local paper.

3. **Staff Development:** The teacher will present a workshop on **Wise Buys** to other teachers at the district math conference.

*Addenda, letter of support, and South Carolina Framework are not included for this example.

Project Title: Motoring on to Learning

Amount Requested: $2,000

Note: *In grant writing, one of the most challenging sections to design is the Justification or Needs Statement section of narrative. This sample is included because it successfully mixes the "anecdotal" evidence of teacher experience with more pragmatic research and demographic data to make a convincing case for funding.*

Each day, I watch my preschool children with special needs trying so hard to do things that "typical" preschool children do. I hear my children asking for play experiences and, unfortunately, I don't have the equipment at my school site for them to get these play experiences.

For example, a few weeks ago, I borrowed an adaptive tricycle from the school district's physical therapy department. I attempted to teach one of my students to ride the tricycle, a child who has cerebral palsy. This child immediately said, "I can't do it, Mrs. Camlin." Knowing that he had never been on a tricycle, I encouraged him, reminding him of his favorite story "The Little Engine That Could." I told him over and over, "I think I can . . . I think I can."

As we practiced riding and repeated the statement, he began to pedal on his own. His little face lit up just as bright as the sun, and he began screaming, "I can!" By the end of the session, he was freely pedaling down the school hallway with a big, bright grin on his face. When he got off the tricycle, he said, "I did an excellent job, Mrs. Camlin." I assured him that he had.

In addition to this kind of real-life evidence for funding **Motoring on to Learning**, research indicates that motor skill development can help build self-esteem in children. The May 1991 issue of the *Elementary School Journal* highlights the importance of movement activities in building self-confidence, which is so critical to special needs children.

Moreover, this article presents the idea that the motor skills of children in the first three grades tend to reflect the types and number of opportunities they have had to develop them. If children spend enough time building gross motor skills, it will also help them build other more academic skills. (Addendum I)*

Looking further, we see that "typical" youngsters at Anyville Elementary School score an average of 20 out of 31 points on the DIAL-R, motor skills section. This is a screening test for young children. However, my special needs children only score an average of 9 out of 31 points in the motor skills area. This test, the *Development Indicators for the Assessment of Learning* gives me evidence that suggests my students are at risk for motor, as well as cognitive, delays. In fact, while only five percent of four-year-old kindergarten students will receive physical therapy, over 50 percent of my students are under a therapist's care. Clearly, I must mix motor skills work with more traditional classroom work in order to meet these children's needs.

Motoring on to Learning will enable me to set up a motor skills center in my classroom, complete with a mini trampoline, kangaroo balls, adaptive tricycles, parachutes, tumbling mats, and bean-bag games. According to Dr. May _____, a local pediatrician who specializes in the care of delayed children, this center will do much to improve the long-term development of these children. Her letter of support is attached. (Addendum II)*

*Addenda are not included for this example.

Project Title: Vis-à-vis Instruction

Funds Requested: $3,235.00

Project Description

When I first started teaching, using the overhead projector was the cutting edge of technology. Today, **Vis-à-vis Instruction** means using the LCD projection panel to demonstrate the steps in the writing process to third graders, or visiting the ocean floor (via CD-ROM) to fifth graders, or instructing a classroom full of parents in using a computer in our parenting room. The LCD projection panel will bring Anyville Elementary School into the forefront of technology and will enhance curriculum and instruction at multiple levels. Our Activities section* demonstrates how this equipment will be implemented in the parenting program and in each grade level from four-year-old child development to sixth grade. **Vis-à-vis Instruction** literally means "eye to eye." Of course, individual instruction is always the ideal, but that is not possible. The use of the LCD projection panel is as close to individual instruction as one can come without great expense and time. Our teacher innovation grant, **Vis-à-vis Instruction**, uses the latest technology to give personalized attention to students of all ages.

Need for the Project

Computer tutorial programs alone are not sufficient to increase reading and math levels of socioeconomically disadvantaged students. Evidence indicates that when students make relevant connections in curriculum, then retention of knowledge is greater (Means, 1994). Research suggests that computer instruction, when used effectively, benefits students (Reinking, 1988).

However, standardized test scores indicate that students who use computers solely for reading and math drill and practice are not receiving the full benefit of learning by integrating technology with thematic topics studied in the classroom. (Addendum I)*

Vis-à-vis Instruction can help students find connections in learning between classroom content and the computer lab.

Anyville Elementary students come from low socioeconomic backgrounds with 96 percent of the students receiving free or reduced-rate lunch. These students' experiences outside the home are limited. It is not always possible to transport students to other locations in order to provide enriching experiences that will enhance their knowledge base. However, **Vis-à-vis Instruction** will bring the experiences to the student through computer technology.

A review of state-mandated test scores (Addendum I)* shows that nearly half of the fourth-grade students and one-third of the fifth-grade students have remained in the bottom quartile. This suggests that students are not benefiting significantly from daily tutorial programs.

Percent in Bottom Quartile		
Metropolitan 7 Achievement Scores		
	Reading	Math
4th Grade—1996	39	44
1997	50	46
5th Grade—1996	37	44
1997	37	30

Mrs. B., media specialist, and Mrs. G., school facilitator, feel their collaboration will bring success to **Vis-à-vis Instruction** through Mrs. B.'s technical expertise and Mrs. G.'s overall knowledge of school curriculum. Special equipment is needed for direct instruction using the computer, and the added benefit of software programs allows technology and curriculum to go hand in hand.

Finally, my proposal has been endorsed by Dr. Linda Karges-Bone, professor, author, and noted grant writer, whose letter of support is attached. (Addendum III)*

Goal, Objectives, and Evaluation Measures

Goal A: The goal of our grant proposal, **Vis-à-vis Instruction**, is to improve teaching practices and procedures by implementing technology that will allow direct instruction with computers to take place. Students will no longer use computers solely for tutorial practice, but will be able to integrate technology with classroom content. Teachers will now have access to motivational and useful software and the equipment necessary to make content areas relevant to thematic units studied in the classroom.

Objective 1: By September 1998, 100 percent of the teachers will be trained to use the LCD projection panel, overhead projector, and software in direct instruction.

Evaluation 1: Teachers will complete the Training Evaluation Sheet (Addendum III)* to evaluate the training and determine their readiness to implement the program.

Objective 2: By May 1999, 85 percent of the student body will receive direct instruction using the LCD projection panel, overhead projector, and designated software.

Evaluation 2: Students will complete surveys to evaluate the effectiveness of the technology on learning and to evaluate individual software programs. (Addendum V)*

Objective 3: By May 1999, 85 percent of the teachers will have integrated direct instruction using technology with at least one thematic unit.

Evaluation 3: After teachers implement the program, they will complete a critique of integrating the technology with thematic units to evaluate the effectiveness of technology on instruction, and to evaluate their students' performance on the lesson assessment.

Objective 4: By May 1999, 85 percent of the parents who receive direct instruction using the LCD projection panel, overhead projector, and software will increase their understanding of computer technology and computer literacy.

Evaluation 4: Parents will complete surveys throughout the school year to evaluate the effectiveness of the technology on learning and to evaluate the software program(s).

Objective 5: In grades four and five, there will be an increase in the number of students above the bottom quartile in reading and math.

Evaluation 5: Test scores will be compared for 1998 and 1999 to determine student gains from the bottom quartile.

Connections to Curriculum Objectives

Goal A: To improve teaching practices and procedures by implementing technology that allows direct instruction with computers to take place, which is consistent with standards in the **Science, Mathematics, and English Language Arts Frameworks** (examples specifically cited below refer to the South Carolina Frameworks).*

The **South Carolina Science Framework** supports the project through standards for learning science by connections to other disciplines and making effective use of technology (pp. 12 and 13).*

The **South Carolina English Language Arts Framework** supports the project through standards for instructional materials and by incorporating technology into the English Language Arts curriculum to enhance reading, writing, and speaking across the curriculum (pp. 62–65).*

The **South Carolina Math Framework** supports the project through standards for K–12 curriculum (p. 34)* that students must encounter math through communication and connections.

Objectives 2 and 4: By May 1999, 85 percent of students will receive instruction and increase their knowledge using the LCD projection panel, the computer, and the software. Specific software programs have been selected that address all major content areas of the curriculum, including science, math, and English language arts.

Objectives 1 and 3: Teachers receive training to properly implement the project.

The **South Carolina Science Framework** supports the project by stating that the framework's foundation is built upon the point that all South Carolina teachers are well prepared to provide relevant, engaging, and accurate science instruction using appropriate methods, materials, and equipment (p. 7).*

The **South Carolina English Language Arts Framework** supports this grant through professional development by establishing teachers as experts (p. 91) and by providing comprehensive training in how to use the technology (p. 65).*

School Renewal Plan, Strategy 2, Objective 1: Establishing programs that foster creativity, develop communication skills, and enhance technical knowledge for students.

Strategy 3, Objective 2: Gains more access to technology through the use of computer systems.

Strategy 4, Objective 5: Enhances media resources to provide academic and personal support for teachers and students.

Objectives 1–5 will address this as teachers receive technology through the media center that will provide more effective direct instruction and foster creativity and communication through the use of software programs and computers.

Project Strategy

Note: Bold-face items are purchased with grant funds.

I. **Preparation**
   Bar code the **LCD projection panel**, **overhead projector**, and **software** in the media center for teachers to check out. A **packet of information** for teachers will be prepared that will describe each piece of **software**, identify appropriate age and grade levels, and suggest ideas for integrating technology with curriculum content.

II. **Explanation of Program**
   A **one-day teacher in-service** will be conducted in August 1998. Mrs. B., media specialist, will train all teachers and assistants at Anyville Elementary on how to operate the *Vis-à-vis Instruction* equipment, which includes the LCD projection panel and overhead projector, and Mrs. G., school facilitator, will review the **software information packets**, conduct demonstrations, and discuss methods for integrating technology with classroom content. **Lunch** will be provided during the in-service.

Mrs. B. will house the equipment and software in the library for checkout by classroom teachers, as needed. Mrs. G. will be available to assist teachers, as needed, to coordinate the technology into classroom instruction in grades from four-year-old child development through sixth grade, and the parenting class.

In class, the *Vis-à-vis Instruction* program will be explained to students prior to the teacher integrating the technology with the thematic unit(s).

III. Program Implementation

As the teachers implement the *Vis-à-vis Instruction* program during the school year, they will complete the evaluation form and turn it in to Mrs. G.

Parents will receive weekly instruction using *Vis-à-vis Instruction.*

Students will complete evaluation forms following instruction with each piece of **software** used. Teachers will turn in all evaluation forms simultaneously upon completion of a particular thematic unit.

Parents will complete evaluation forms for each different piece of **software** used.

IV. Software Components of the Program

The **software** addresses the following objectives and can be used in some cases by more than one grade level.

1. Adult Computer Class—demonstrates word processing and desktop publishing

2. Four-year-old Child Development—communicates orally

3. Five-year-old Kindergarten—classifies objects

4. First Grade—appreciates literature

5. Second Grade—writes original stories

6. Third Grade—observes and records information

7. Fourth Grade—discusses and observes space exploration

8. Fifth Grade—explores oceans

9. Sixth Grade—researches data and writes reports

Time Line for the Project

August | Order materials. Hold teacher in-service. Schedule teachers to videotape. Determine schedule for adult computer class, and notify parents.

September | Implement direct instruction using technology.

October | Document use of technology after first nine weeks. Report in school newsletter and make any necessary adjustments. Collect lesson plans from appropriate grade levels. Schedule teachers to videotape during second nine weeks.

January | Document use of technology for second nine weeks. Update report for newsletter. Collect lesson plans from appropriate grade levels. Schedule teachers to videotape during third nine weeks.

March | Document use of technology for third nine weeks. Update newsletter. Collect lesson plans from appropriate grade levels.

April | Have remaining grade levels complete critiques. Have parents and remaining students complete surveys.

May | Compile results of all feedback to determine strengths and weaknesses of program. Compile final report with Metropolitan 7 Achievement Test scores. Compile and publish lesson-plan book. Share final results with faculty and staff.

Dissemination of Information and Exportable Products

The exportable products for **Vis-à-vis Instruction** will be:

1. A published book that contains sample lesson plans from teachers who have successfully integrated technology with thematic units. This book will be used by other teachers for future curriculum planning.

2. A videotape of teachers who implement direct instruction using the LCD projection panel, overhead projector, computer, and software.

3. Data from the surveys will be compiled to determine positive and negative feedback from teachers, parents, and students. The data will be shared with the faculty to determine necessary changes in the program.

4. News articles will be submitted to local newspapers, highlighting the program.

*Addenda, activities, and the South Carolina Frameworks are not included for this example.

Budget for Vis-à-vis Instruction

Equipment

Atlaz International LTD
616 Burnside Avenue
P.O. Box 960110
Inwood, NY 11096-0110
Fax: 1-888-437-3329

Infocus LCD Projection Panel Smartview 3600	$1,729.00
Overhead Projector 4000 Lumen (required to run LCD panel)	790.00
Shipping and Handling Free	
TOTAL:	$2,519.00

Software

National School Products
Attn: Dept. W
101 East Broadway
Maryville, TN 37804-2498
(423) 984-3960
Fax: 1-800-289-3960

Learn to Do Desktop Publishing	$40.00
Let's Start Learning	50.00
Marty and the Trouble with Cheese	50.00
The Greatest Children's Stories Ever Told	50.00
My Own Stories	20.00
Encyclopedia of Nature	60.00
Space and Astronomy	40.00
Oceans Below	40.00
Bookshelf 95	70.00
Subtotal	420.00
Shipping and Handling 5%	21.00
TOTAL:	$441.00

Training

One-day staff development with lunch provided $250.00

Software information packets   25.00
(paper and printing)

TOTAL: $275.00

TOTAL EXPENDITURES: **$3,235.00**

Project Title: Art Smart

Funds Requested: $2,000.00

Rationale for and Description of the Project

The project **Art Smart** is a program to increase students' knowledge of art, artists, and cultures through the use of reading, writing, and responding to visual resources. This grant will impact kindergarten through second grade at Anyville Elementary School in Anywhere County. This project will provide our at-risk students with a motivational way to increase academic skills and knowledge of art. Students will participate in written work and verbal discussions of art imagery. Students will use many critical thinking skills to interpret works of art. Special emphasis will be placed on gaining knowledge of multicultural art, especially African American art.

Anyville Elementary School offers an ideal canvas on which to paint an innovative arts program that improves basic skills. This large (840 students), ethnically diverse school has a population that is 45 percent minority students, of which 60 percent receive free or reduced-rate lunch. This means that our students are likely to be at risk for a variety of social and educational delays. My grant, **Art Smart**, has school-wide emphasis on language and aesthetics through the various artistic media.

According to the South Carolina Frameworks for the Arts, quality "arts education facilitates human communication and literacy within and across cultures." Additional findings from the Getty Center for Education in the Arts emphasizes imagery as a central part of language formation (Addendum I)*, another part of my grant.

Moreover, my original research, done in the form of an "Art Skills Review" demonstrates limited knowledge of content in the arts. (Addendum II)* For example, 42 percent of second graders could not describe differences in types of art.

Teachers at Anyville Elementary stated that students had problems making comparisons and finding differences and similarities.

The state frameworks refer to the need for cultural diversity. "A quality art program engages in the study of art from diverse time periods, cultures, and ethnic groups" (pg. 2)*.

In summation, the program **Art Smart** will impact 840 students and will improve their language and aesthetic skills while increasing students' knowledge of art and the ability to interpret it.

Finally, a letter of support from Susan E___, Gibbes Museum of Art, shows the critical need for this grant.*

Goals, Objectives, and Evaluation Measures

The goals of the project **Art Smart** are to strengthen the discipline-based art curriculum through the use of visual resources in accordance to the South Carolina Frameworks for the Arts.

1. By the end of the school year, students in grades K–2 will be able to achieve 75 percent accuracy in recognizing artists, styles, and subject matter for their grade level.

2. By the end of the school year, students will be able to identify, analyze, and appreciate art from different cultures with 75 percent accuracy.

3. Students will keep a journal for written and visual responses. By the end of the year, students will increase verbal/written and/or drawn responses of works of art by 50 percent. Students will use skills of interpretation, differentiation, analysis, and judgment.

4. Students will travel to the Gibbes Museum of Art in Charleston, South Carolina, to experience an art gallery and create a work of art while at the museum.

5. By the end of the school year, students will be able to use art vocabulary effectively, think critically about art, and write about works of art.

As the South Carolina Frameworks for the Arts notes, "Arts education encourages divergent thinking through problem-solving creativity. Classroom evidence suggest that the strengths gained through a comprehensive study of the arts carries over into other subject areas" (pg. 1)*.

The **Art Smart** project goals will strengthen the curriculum in the arts in accordance with the South Carolina Frameworks for the Arts. "The scope of arts education has expanded beyond a focus on performance and production to a more balanced study of aesthetics, performance/production, history/culture, and criticism. In addition, educators have broadened their views of the arts, from a perspective defined by western civilization to a more worldwide understanding that encompasses diverse cultural and ethnic groups" (pg. 3)*.

"In keeping with this broader view of arts education, the four previously-developed state arts education documents are organized around a common set of curricular components— aesthetic perception, creative expression, historical and cultural heritage, and aesthetic valuing. These four components form the basis for a comprehensive education in the arts" (pg. 4)*.

Relationship of Objectives to the State Curriculum

The relationship of the objectives of **Art Smart** are directly related to that of our school's Strategic Plan under Strategy 1, which is "to develop and implement a curriculum in the arts using hands-on exploratory experiences to problem solve." For example, during their field trip to the Gibbes Museum of Art, students will interpret, analyze, and judge many varied and unusual types of art, as well as create a work of art based on their experiences at the museum.

The South Carolina Frameworks for the Arts notes, "Art education encourages divergent thinking skills through problem solving and creativity." The **Art Smart** goals will strengthen the curriculum in accordance to the South Carolina Frameworks for the Arts by giving students visual problems to solve throughout the year. For example:

Second Grade. Students will be introduced to various impressionist artists such as Van Gogh, Seurat, Monet, and Childe Hassam. Students will then be asked to create a painting based on the styles of the various impressionist artists. Background information will be given about the artists, and several demonstrations of differing techniques will be shown.

First Grade. Students will be introduced to Leonardo Da Vinci, given historical background, and shown various works of his art. Students will then listen to *The Very Hungry Caterpillar* by Eric Carle (Putnam Publishing Group, 1994). Metamorphosis will be discussed, as well as how Da Vinci changed inventions and works of art he created. Students will then problem-solve and create a collage based on metamorphosis.

These are just a few examples of how the **Art Smart** project will be implemented, and how it relates to the State Frameworks and our school Strategic Plan.

Program Strategy/Activities

Students will participate in **Art Smart** activities weekly in art class. During the first 10 to 15 minutes of class, students will view or examine artwork using either reproductions, laser disc/television, or cultural art kits. Students will learn historical information about the artists and cultures, and participate orally or in writing. Many critical-thinking questions will be used (interpretation, differentiation, discrimination, analysis, and judgment).

Sample Activities

1. Comparing two works of art by the same artist (Henri Matisse cutouts)

2. Interpreting the mood of the work of art based on art elements (prints)

3. Describing works of art (art books)

4. Describing a visual story on the student's interpretation of the work of art

5. Describing specific elements and concepts within a work of art (art books)

6. Comparing two works of art by separate artists (Jacob Lawrence vs. Jonathan Green)

7. Learning historical data on artists and cultures through cultural art kits

8. Identifying subject matter and themes in a work of art (art prints)

9. Describing personal likes and dislikes in specific works of art (prints/laser disc)

10. Analyzing a work of art using specific concepts (art prints)

11. Making judgments on works of art (laser disc/prints)

12. Comparing concepts used in famous works of art to their own art (laser disc)

13. Traveling on a field trip to the Gibbes Museum of Art in Charleston. There students will be given the opportunity to orally respond to original works of art and understand the difference between reproductions and the original art. They will also be given the opportunity to create a work of art based on visual stimulation at the museum.

Time Line for the Project

July 1997	Order materials.
August 1997–May 1998	Weekly art discussions and activities
September 1997	Pretest
September 1997	Record observational and anecdotal data; write visual responses in art journals.
November 1997	Field trip to art museum
May 1998	Final test on art concepts; gather data for multicultural instruction using grade book; assess student portfolios
June 1998	Final budget report; project summary

Evaluation Plan

1. Recognition of artist, styles, and subject matter will be measured with a teacher-made pretest in September and a final test in May. Success will be achieved if students can name artists, styles, and subject matter, and respond to works of art with 75 percent accuracy.

2. To measure multicultural awareness, the teacher will gather observational and anecdotal data. Observational data will be collected during class time using a grade book to record student responses. Success will be achieved if students respond with 75 percent accuracy.

3. A checklist of skills will be given to parents twice a year. (Addendum III)*

4. Students will write about their trip to the Gibbes Museum in their art journals.

5. To measure art vocabulary, to write about works of art, and to think critically about art, the teacher will give a test in May. Success will be achieved if students can use art vocabulary, write about artwork, and give critical responses about art with 75 percent accuracy.

6. The teacher will complete a resource book that will give background information on artists and cultures. References for the laser disc will be listed for easy access. Included will be a list of week-by-week critical-thinking questions to use for each specific work of art. The teacher and students will create big books analyzing art and giving background information on artists and cultures, with student interpretations/variations of the various cultures and artists studied.

7. Students will collect their written/visual responses in a student journal. At the end of May, a sample group will be assessed for a 50 percent increase in written/visual responses and the ability to use critical-thinking skills. Verbal responses will be recorded in a teacher grade book to measure participation and accuracy for the year, and will be compared to responses from the beginning of the year.

Description/Dissemination of Information and Exportable Product

1. The project coordinator will share her results and samples of student work at the school district's "Teacher Fair" in February.

2. The students' works of art that they create, their journals, and art book will all be items they will be able to keep throughout the year.

*Addenda, letter of support, and South Carolina State Frameworks are not included for this example.

Notes

Notes